Forgotten Treasures

This collection first published in 2007
by Express Newspapers
The Northern & Shell Building
Number 10 Lower Thames Street
London EC3R 6EN

ISBN 9 7808 5079 3786

Cover design & typesetting by Sarah Reed

Printed and bound in Poland by Polskabook

DAILY EXPRESS

Forgotten Treasures

Compiled by William Hartston

The Daily Express

CONTENTS

INTRODUCTION

'Poetry is the spontaneous overflow of powerful feelings: it takes its origin from emotion recollected in tranquillity.'
William Wordsworth

In the spring of 2006, a reader wrote to the *Daily Express* Saturday Briefing page to ask if we could identify a poem for her. All Ros Hinks could remember were the lines, 'But I have promises to keep, And miles to go before I sleep'. We identified it as 'Stopping By Woods On A Snowy Evening' by the American poet Robert Frost, and sent her a copy of the poem. When we published her query and the answer, dozens of letters followed asking 'Can I have a copy too', and dozens more letters with requests to trace poetry dimly remembered from schooldays. Just a mention of the poem had been enough to awaken memories of the emotions felt when learning or reading it, decades earlier.

A few weeks later, the same thing happened with a request from Belinda Brown of Cambridge: 'When I was young, my father used to recite a poem to me starting, "I once had a beautiful doll, dears, The most beautiful doll in the world". I have never been able to find this poem anywhere. Please help.' How could we refuse? We quickly discovered that Belinda had slightly misquoted the verse. It was a 'sweet little doll' not a beautiful one, in Charles Kingsley's poem, 'The Lost Doll'. This time, there were even more letters from readers asking for a copy. 'My mother used to recite this over sixty years ago,' Eunice Pooley wrote from Barnsley. 'I had never heard it since then until I saw it in your column.' Once more we were deluged with requests for the poem and pleas to identify more verse snippets. So we gave Forgotten Verse its own slot on the Saturday Briefing page, and began by printing the whole of Kingsley's poem. 'It evoked so many happy memories,' Chris Young of Banbury wrote gratefully. 'I can still hear my mother reciting it to me sixty years ago.'

Giving Forgotten Verse its own space led to even more requests. When I complained to *Daily Express* editor Peter Hill that I was having to deal with 150 letters a week on lost poems alone, his response was immediate: 'Then we must do it daily.'

Several thousand reader letters later, we are still hunting down verses and, to judge from the numerous appreciative responses, rekindling those powerful feelings to which Wordsworth referred. Many of the requests are beautifully written letters from readers in their eighties or even nineties, often searching for poems they remember hearing on a grandmother's knees and now wanting to treat their own grandchildren – or in more than one case, great-grandchildren – to the same experience.

This collection is in response to the hundreds of you who have asked: 'When are you going to bring out an anthology of Forgotten Verse?' I hope you all enjoy re-discovering long-lost verses, and perhaps making a few new friends from those you may not have heard before. Many of the poems in this book have appeared in the pages of the *Daily Express* and I have taken the opportunity to include a few longer ones for which we have insufficient space in the paper.

If you are wondering why your own favourite is not included, the answer may simply be that we have not got round to it yet – there is a long queue for this space – or it may be for reasons of copyright. That is why we have no Walter de la Mare, John Masefield, John Betjeman or Henry Newbolt, all of whose poems have been requested on numerous occasions. Nevertheless, I am sure you will find enough here to satisfy your poetic appetite. From war to whimsy, from horror to humour, from love to leisure, *Daily Express* readers have heard it all, in verse, at school or soon after, and we hope this book will play its part in nudging some of those fond memories back into existence.

I am very grateful to all the readers who have written in to the paper with their requests for awakening my own interest in poetry out of a long slumber, and special thanks are due to Vicky Reed and Fiona Tucker of Express Books for nurturing this project through so patiently, and to Neil Richards for his hugely valuable contribution to this whole project while doing work experience at the *Daily Express*.

William Hartston
Daily Express, London EC3
February 2007.

1.

Nostalgia

THE LITTLE DOLL
by Charles Kingsley

I once had a sweet little doll, dears,
　The prettiest doll in the world;
Her cheeks were so red and so white, dears,
　And her hair was so charmingly curled.

But I lost my poor little doll, dears
　As I played in the heath one day;
And I cried for her more than a week, dears,
　But I never could find where she lay.

I found my poor little doll, dears,
　As I played in the heath one day;
Folks say she is terrible changed, dears,
　For her paint is all washed away,
And her arm trodden off by the cows, dears,
　And her hair not the least bit curled;
Yet for old sakes' sake she is still, dears,
　The prettiest doll in the world.

Charles Kingsley (1819–75)
Best known for his classic children's story The Water Babies *and
the novel* Westward Ho!*, Kingsley also wrote some fine poetry.
He was Professor of Modern History at Cambridge University.*

AFTERNOON IN FEBRUARY
by Henry Wadsworth Longfellow

The day is ending,
The night is descending;
The marsh is frozen,
The river dead.
Through clouds like ashes
The red sun flashes
On village windows
That glimmer red.

The snow recommences;
The buried fences
Mark no longer
The road o'er the plain;
While through the meadows,
Like fearful shadows,
Slowly passes
A funeral train.

The bell is pealing,
And every feeling
Within me responds
To the dismal knell;
Shadows are trailing,
My heart is bewailing
And tolling within
Like a funeral bell.

Henry Wadsworth Longfellow (1807–82)
Longfellow's simple and clear-cut verse made him a favourite
both in his home country of the United States and in Britain. His
epic poems such as 'Hiawatha' and 'Paul Revere's Ride' helped
to establish American mythology. At his death he became the first
American poet to be honoured with a bust in Poets' Corner at
Westminster Abbey.

THE GRAVES OF A HOUSEHOLD
by Felicia Dorothea Hemans

They grew in beauty, side by side,
They fill'd one home with glee;–
Their graves are sever'd, far and wide,
By mount, and stream, and sea.

The same fond mother bent at night
O'er each fair sleeping brow;
She had each folded flower in sight,–
Where are those dreamers now?

One, midst the forests of the west,
By a dark stream is laid,–
The Indian knows his place of rest,
Far in the cedar shade.

The sea, the blue lone sea, hath one,
He lies where pearls lie deep;
He was the lov'd of all, yet none
O'er his low bed may weep.

One sleeps where southern vines are drest
Above the noble slain:
He wrapt his colours round his breast,
On a blood-red field of Spain.

And one–o'er her the myrtle showers
Its leaves, by soft winds fann'd;
She faded midst Italian flowers,–
The last of that bright band.

And parted thus they rest, who play'd
Beneath the same green tree;
Whose voices mingled as they pray'd
Around one parent knee!

They that with smiles lit up the hall,
And cheer'd with song the hearth,–
Alas! for love, if thou wert all,
And nought beyond, oh earth!

Felicia Dorothea Hemans (1793–1835)
*Born in Liverpool, the granddaughter to an Italian consul to the
city, but brought up in Wales, Felicia Hemans was a celebrated
poet of her time, but is now mainly remembered for just one line,
'The boy stood on the burning deck' (from 'Casabianca',
included later in this collection).*

*The above verse was requested by Mrs T Black of
Dumfriesshire who told us her Dad used to recite a poem to her,
beginning, 'They grew in beauty side by side'.*

THE BEGINNING
by Rupert Brooke

Some day I shall rise and leave my friends
And seek you again through the world's far ends,
You whom I found so fair
(Touch of your hands and smell of your hair!),
My only god in the days that were.
My eager feet shall find you again,
Though the sullen years and the mark of pain
Have changed you wholly; for I shall know
(How could I forget having loved you so?),
In the sad half-light of evening,
The face that was all my sunrising.
So then at the ends of the earth I'll stand
And hold you fiercely by either hand,
And seeing your age and ashen hair
I'll curse the thing that once you were,
Because it is changed and pale and old
(Lips that were scarlet, hair that was gold!),
And I loved you before you were old and wise,
When the flame of youth was strong in your eyes,
And my heart is sick with memories.

Rupert Brooke (1887–1915)
*Described by fellow poet W B Yeats as 'the handsomest young
man in England', Rupert Brooke has often been portrayed as the
very model of a romantic young poet tragically cut down in war
time – yet he only saw one day's action in the First World War
and died of septicaemia brought on by a mosquito bite. His
poetry, however, had a powerful simplicity, and his early death
earned him the remarkable tribute of an obituary in* The Times
newspaper written by Winston Churchill himself.

TIME'S PACES
by Henry Twells

When as a child I laughed and wept,
Time crept.
When as a youth I waxed more bold,
Time strolled.
When I became a full-grown man,
Time RAN.
When older still I daily grew,
Time FLEW.
Soon I shall find, in passing on,
Time gone.
O Christ! wilt Thou have saved me then?
Amen.

Henry Twells (1823–1900)
Headmaster of Godolphin School in Hammersmith, London, then
vicar of Waltham on the Wolds, Leicestershire and Canon of
Peterborough in 1884, Twells is best known as a hymn-writer, but
as this poem exemplifies, he wrote the occasional religious verse
as well.

THE DARK-EYED GENTLEMAN
by Thomas Hardy

I pitched my day's leazings in Crimmercrock Lane,
To tie up my garter and jog on again,
When a dear dark-eyed gentleman passed there and said,
In a way that made all o' me colour rose-red,
"What do I see—
O pretty knee!"
And he came and he tied up my garter for me.

'Twixt sunset and moonrise it was, I can mind:
Ah, 'tis easy to lose what we nevermore find!—
Of the dear stranger's home, of his name, I knew nought,
But I soon knew his nature and all that it brought.
Then bitterly
Sobbed I that he
Should ever have tied up my garter for me!

Yet now I've beside me a fine lissom lad,
And my slip's nigh forgot, and my days are not sad;
My own dearest joy is he, comrade, and friend,
He it is who safe-guards me, on him I depend;
No sorrow brings he,
And thankful I be
That his daddy once tied up my garter for me!

Thomas Hardy (1840–1928)
Best known for his novels such as Tess of the D'Urbervilles, *set
in the fictional county of Wessex, Hardy maintained that his first
love was poetry, which he continued to produce throughout his
life.*

The poem is from a collection called Time's Laughingstocks
and Other Verses. *'Leazings', incidentally, means a bundle of
gleaned corn.*

LONGING
by Matthew Arnold

Come to me in my dreams, and then
By day I shall be well again!
For so the night will more than pay
The hopeless longing of the day.
Come, as thou cam'st a thousand times,
A messenger from radiant climes,
And smile on thy new world, and be
As kind to others as to me!
Or, as thou never cam'st in sooth,
Come now, and let me dream it truth,
And part my hair, and kiss my brow,
And say, My love why sufferest thou?
Come to me in my dreams, and then
By day I shall be well again!
For so the night will more than pay
The hopeless longing of the day.

Matthew Arnold (1822–88)
Poet, literary critic and schools inspector, Matthew Arnold was
the son of Thomas Arnold, the headmaster of Rugby School
celebrated in the novel Tom Brown's Schooldays. Appointed
Professor of Poetry at Oxford, he repaid the honour by coining
the term 'dreaming spires' which has been applied to the
University ever since.

THE YELLOW DAFFODIL
by Horace Smith

Grey was the morn, all things were grey
'Twas winter more than spring;
A bleak east wind swept o'er the land
And sobered everything.
Grey was the sky, the fields were grey,
The hills, the woods, the trees –
Distance and foreground – all the scene
Was grey in the grey breeze.
Grey cushions, and a grey skin rug,
A dark grey wicker trap,
Grey was the ladies' hats and cloaks,
And grey my coat and cap.
A narrow, lonely, grey old lane,
And lo, on a grey gate,
Just by the side of a grey wood,
A sooty sweep there sat!
With grimy chin 'twixt grimy hands
He sat and whistled shrill;
And in his sooty cap he wore
A yellow daffodil.

And often when the days are dull,
I seem to see him still –
The jaunty air, the sooty face –
And the yellow daffodil.

Horace Smith (1779–1849)
Certainly the only poet in this collection who was also a
prosperous stockbroker, Horace Smith was a friend of Shelley,
who wrote of him, 'Is it not odd that the only truly generous
person I ever knew who had money enough to be generous with
should be a stockbroker?'

ADLESTROP
by Edward Thomas

Yes. I remember Adlestrop –
The name, because one afternoon
Of heat the express-train drew up there
Unwontedly. It was late June.

The steam hissed.
Someone cleared his throat.
No one left and no one came
On the bare platform. What I saw
Was Adlestrop – only the name.

And willows, willow-herb, and grass,
And meadowsweet, and haycocks dry,
No whit less still and lonely fair
Than the high cloudlets in the sky.

And for that minute a blackbird sang
Close by, and round him, mistier,
Farther and farther, all the birds
Of Oxfordshire and Gloucestershire.

Edward Thomas (1878–1917)
Despite being almost forty and a married man, which could have
earned him exemption from enlisting in the army, Edward
Thomas volunteered to serve in the Artists' Rifles and was killed
in action at Arras in France. He wrote a few poems about the
war, but is best remembered for his affectionate evocation of the
English countryside.

Adlestrop Railway Station in Gloucestershire was closed in
1966, but the station bench can still be seen in the village,
complete with Edward Thomas's poem engraved on a plaque.

A SMUGGLER'S SONG
by Rudyard Kipling

If you wake at midnight, and hear a horse's feet,
Don't go drawing back the blind, or looking in the street.
Them that ask no questions isn't told a lie.
Watch the wall, my darling, while the Gentlemen go by!

Five and twenty ponies,
Trotting through the dark –
Brandy for the Parson,
'Baccy for the Clerk;
Laces for a lady, letters for a spy,
And watch the wall, my darling, while the Gentlemen go by!

Running round the woodlump, if you chance to find
Little barrels, roped and tarred, all full of brandy-wine,
Don't you shout to come and look, nor use 'em for your play.
Put the brishwood back again - and they'll be gone next day!
If you see the stable-door setting open wide;
If you see a tired horse lying down inside;
If your mother mends a coat cut about and tore;
If the lining's wet and warm – don't you ask no more!

If you meet King George's men, dressed in blue and red,
You be careful what you say, and mindful what is said.
If they call you 'pretty maid,' and chuck you 'neath the chin,
Don't you tell where no one is, nor yet where no one's been!

Knocks and footsteps round the house – whistles after dark –
You've no call for running out until the house dogs bark.
Trusty's here, and Pincher's here, and see how dumb they lie –
They don't fret to follow when the Gentlemen go by!

If you do as you've been told, likely there's a chance,
You'll be given a dainty doll, all the way from France,
With a cap of Valenciennes, and a velvet hood –
A present from the Gentlemen, along o' being good!

Five and twenty ponies,
Trotting through the dark –
Brandy for the Parson,
'Baccy for the Clerk;
Them that asks no questions isn't told a lie –
Watch the wall, my darling, while the Gentlemen go by.

Rudyard Kipling (1865–1936)
*Born in British India, Kipling became one of the best story-
tellers and writers of patriotic verse Britain has known. He won
the Nobel Prize for Literature in 1907 – the first British recipient
of that prize and still the youngest ever to be so honoured – but
he turned down both a knighthood and an invitation to become
Poet Laureate. He is best known for his stirring verse and for
writing* The Jungle Book *and the* Just So Stories *for children.
This poem has been requested by numerous readers, all of whom
remember the last line, but sometimes nothing else.*

LITTLE BOY BLUE
by Eugene Field

The little toy dog is covered with dust,
But sturdy and stanch he stands;
And the little toy soldier is red with rust,
And his musket moulds in his hands.
Time was when the little toy dog was new,
And the soldier was passing fair;
And that was the time when our Little Boy Blue
Kissed them and put them there.

'Now, don't you go till I come,' he said,
'And don't you make any noise!'
So, toddling off to his trundle-bed,
He dreamt of the pretty toys;
And, as he was dreaming, an angel song
Awakened our Little Boy Blue –
Oh! the years are many, the years are long,
But the little toy friends are true!

Ay, faithful to Little Boy Blue they stand,
Each in the same old place –
Awaiting the touch of a little hand,
The smile of a little face;
And they wonder, as waiting the long years through
In the dust of that little chair,
What has become of our Little Boy Blue,
Since he kissed them and put them there.

Eugene Field (1850–95)
A humorous writer and children's poet, Eugene Field worked as
a journalist in St Louis and Chicago. Poems such as this one
gained him such popularity that he became known as 'The
Children's Poet'.

AT NIGHT
by Alice Meynell

Home, home from the horizon far and clear,
Hither the soft wings sweep;
Flocks of the memories of the day draw near
The dovecote doors of sleep.
O which are they that come through sweetest light
Of all these homing birds?
Which with the straightest and the swiftest flight?
Your words to me, your words!

Alice Meynell (1847–1922)
*Editor, writer and campaigner for women's suffrage, Alice
Meynell was a tireless contributor to a large number of
periodicals, including the Weekly Register, which her husband
edited, while also bringing up eight children. Her* Collected
Poems, *published in 1913, received such acclaim that she was
even mentioned as a possible Poet Laureate.*

ALADDIN
by James Russell Lowell

When I was a beggarly boy,
And lived in a cellar damp,
I had not a friend nor a toy
But I had Aladdin's lamp.

When I could not sleep for the cold,
I had fire enough in my brain,
And builded with roofs of gold,
My beautiful castles in Spain!

Since then I have toiled day and night,
I have money and power good store,
But I'd give all my lamps of silver bright
For the one that is mine no more.

Take, Fortune, whatever you choose,
You gave and may snatch again,
I have nothing 'twould pain me to lose,
For I own no more castles in Spain!

James Russell Lowell (1819–91)
Poet, critic, satirist and diplomat, Lowell was a leading figure in American literature and became Professor of Modern Languages at Harvard University. In 1877, he was appointed Minister Resident at the Court of Spain, which may explain the reference to 'castles in Spain'.

2.

Pastoral

COMPOSED UPON WESTMINSTER BRIDGE, SEPTEMBER 3, 1802
by William Wordsworth

Earth has not anything to show more fair:
Dull would he be of soul who could pass by
A sight so touching in its majesty:
This City now doth, like a garment, wear
The beauty of the morning; silent, bare,
Ships, towers, domes, theatres, and temples lie
Open unto the fields, and to the sky;
All bright and glittering in the smokeless air.
Never did sun more beautifully steep
In his first splendour, valley, rock, or hill;
Ne'er saw I, never felt, a calm so deep!
The river glideth at his own sweet will:
Dear God! the very houses seem asleep;
And all that mighty heart is lying still!

William Wordsworth (1770–1850)
Wordsworth was not only one of the founders of English
Romantic poetry, but he wrote around twice as much as any other
major poet. He was appointed Poet Laureate in 1843, but wrote
practically nothing thereafter.

This poem was requested by Mr D Franey of London: 'I can
remember every word of Wordsworth's 'Daffodils', but his sonnet
on Westminster Bridge escapes me.'

Mr Franey was not alone: the people who put up the London
Eye also forgot the verse. When the wheel was opened, a copy of
this poem was etched on a plaque with lines twelve and thirteen
botched together as 'The river glideth at his own sweet asleep.'
They have put it right now, but they say that it took 830,000 rides
before anyone noticed.

TO DAISIES, NOT TO SHUT SO SOON
by Robert Herrick

Shut not so soon; the dull-eyed night
Has not as yet begun
To make a seizure on the light,
Or to seal up the sun.

No marigolds yet closèd are,
No shadows great appear;
Nor doth the early shepherd's star
Shine like a spangle here.

Stay but till my Julia close
Her life-begetting eye,
And let the whole world then dispose
Itself to live or die.

Robert Herrick (1591–1674)
*One of the most romantic poets of his or any other age, Herrick
was chaplain to the Duke of Buckingham and remained a
bachelor all his life.*

FLOWER CHORUS
by Ralph Waldo Emerson

Such a commotion under the ground,
When March called, 'Ho there! ho!'
Such spreading of rootlets far and wide,
Such whisperings to and fro!
'Are you ready?' the Snowdrop asked,
''Tis time to start, you know.'
'Almost, my dear!' the Scilla replied,
'I'll follow as soon as you go.'
Then 'Ha! ha! ha!' a chorus came
Of laughter sweet and low,
From millions of flowers under the ground,
Yes, millions beginning to grow.

'I'll promise my blossoms,' the Crocus said,
When I hear the blackbird sing.
And straight thereafter, Narcissus cried,
'My silver and gold I'll bring.'
'And ere they are dulled,' another spoke,
'The Hyacinth bells shall ring.'
But the Violet only murmured, 'I'm here'
And sweet grew the air of Spring.

O the pretty brave things, thro' the coldest days
Imprisoned in walls of brown,
They never lost heart tho' the blast shrieked loud,
And the sleet and the hail came down;
But patiently each wrought her wonderful dress,
Or fashioned her beautiful crown,
And now they are coming to lighten the world
Still shadowed by winter's frown.
And well may they cheerily laugh 'Ha! ha!
In laughter sweet and low,
The millions of flowers under the ground,
Yes, millions beginning to grow.

Ralph Waldo Emerson (1803–82)
Essayist, poet, philosopher and schoolmaster, Emerson was one
of the leading intellectuals of nineteenth-century America. Asked
late in life to summarise his work, he said that his central
doctrine was 'the infinitude of the private man'. He wanted no
followers, but to encourage self-reliance in others.

THE BEANFIELD
by John Clare

A bean field full in blossom smells as sweet
As Araby, or groves of orange flowers;
Black-eyed and white, and feathered to one's feet,
How sweet they smell in the morning's dewy hours!
When seething night is left upon the flowers,
And when morn's bright sun shines o'er the field,
The bean-bloom glitters in the gems o' showers,
And sweet the fragrance which the union yields
To battered footpaths crossing o'er the fields.

John Clare (1793–1864)
Known as 'the Northamptonshire Peasant Poet', John Clare was
the son of a farm labourer. Despite very little formal education,
he became a successful and well-respected poet. For some years
in his later life, however, he was confined to a mental asylum and
suffered from delusions including claiming that he had written
the works of Shakespeare.

THE LAST ROSE OF SUMMER
by Thomas Moore

'Tis the last rose of summer,
left blooming all alone;
All her lovely companions
are faded and gone;
No flower of her kindred,
no rose bud is nigh
To reflect back her blushes,
to give sigh for sigh.

I'll not leave thee, thou lone one!
To pine on the stem
Since the lovely are sleeping,
Go sleep thou with them.
Thus kindly I scatter
Thy leaves o'er the bed,
Where thy mates of the garden
Lie scentless and dead.

So soon may I follow,
when friendships decay
And from Love's shining circle
The gems drop away
When true hearts lie withered
And fond ones are flown
Oh! who would inhabit
This bleak world alone!

Thomas Moore (1779–1852)
Born in Dublin, Moore had an extraordinary career, studying law at Trinity College, Dublin and Middle Temple in London before finding fame as a balladeer and singer, and also serving as registrar to the Admiralty in Bermuda.

TRAVEL
by Robert Louis Stevenson

I should like to rise and go
Where the golden apples grow;–
Where below another sky
Parrot islands anchored lie,
And, watched by cockatoos and goats,
Lonely Crusoes building boats;–
Where in sunshine reaching out
Eastern cities, miles about,
Are with mosque and minaret
Among sandy gardens set,
And the rich goods from near and far
Hang for sale in the bazaar;–
Where the Great Wall round China goes,
And on one side the desert blows,
And with the voice and bell and drum,
Cities on the other hum;–
Where are forests hot as fire,
Wide as England, tall as a spire,
Full of apes and cocoa-nuts
And the negro hunters' huts;–
Where the knotty crocodile
Lies and blinks in the Nile,
And the red flamingo flies
Hunting fish before his eyes;–
Where in jungles near and far,
Man-devouring tigers are,
Lying close and giving ear
Lest the hunt be drawing near,
Or a comer-by be seen
Swinging in the palanquin;–
Where among the desert sands
Some deserted city stands,

All its children, sweep and prince,
Grown to manhood ages since,
Not a foot in street or house,
Not a stir of child or mouse,
And when kindly falls the night,
In all the town no spark of light.
There I'll come when I'm a man
With a camel caravan;
Light a fire in the gloom
Of some dusty dining room;
See the pictures on the walls,
Heroes, fights and festivals;
And in a corner find the toys
Of the old Egyptian boys.

Robert Louis Stevenson (1850–94)
Stevenson is renowned for producing such imaginative novels as
Treasure Island *and* The Strange Case of Dr Jekyll and Mr Hyde.
*He also wrote a delightful collection of over sixty short poems
called* A Child's Garden of Verses.

A MUSICAL INSTRUMENT
by Elizabeth Barrett Browning

What was he doing, the great god Pan,
　　Down in the reeds by the river?
Spreading ruin and scattering ban,
Splashing and paddling with hoofs of a goat,
And breaking the golden lilies afloat
　　With the dragon-fly on the river.

He tore out a reed, the great god Pan,
　　From the deep cool bed of the river:
　　The limpid water turbidly ran,
　　And the broken lilies a-dying lay,
　　And the dragon-fly had fled away,
　　Ere he brought it out of the river.

High on the shore sat the great god Pan,
　　While turbidly flowed the river;
And hacked and hewed as a great god can,
With his hard bleak steel at the patient reed,
Till there was not a sign of a leaf indeed
　　To prove it fresh from the river.

He cut it short, did the great god Pan,
　　(How tall it stood in the river!)
Then drew the pith, like the heart of a man,
　　Steadily from the outside ring,
And notched the poor dry empty thing
　　In holes, as he sat by the river.

'This is the way,' laughed the great god Pan,
Laughed while he sat by the river,
'The only way, since gods began
To make sweet music, they could succeed.'
Then, dropping his mouth to a hole in the reed,
He blew in power by the river.

Sweet, sweet, sweet, O Pan!
Piercing sweet by the river!
Blinding sweet, O great god Pan!
The sun on the hill forgot to die,
And the lilies revived, and the dragon-fly
Came back to dream on the river.

Yet half a beast is the great god Pan,
To laugh as he sits by the river,
Making a poet out of a man:
The true gods sigh for the cost and pain, –
For the reed which grows nevermore again
As a reed with the reeds in the river.

Elizabeth Barrett Browning (1806–61)
The greatest British poetess of the nineteenth century, Elizabeth
Barrett Browning was born into a wealthy family in Durham in
1806. She was a direct descendant of Edward III. Because of
poor health as a child, she was educated at home and published
her first poems at the age of fourteen. Her marriage to Robert
Browning in 1846 was one of the great romances, and great
literary partnerships, in history.

BEGGARS' HOLIDAY
by John Fletcher

Cast our caps and cares away,
This is beggars' holiday.
At the crowning of our king,
Thus we ever dance and sing.
In the world look out and see,
Where so happy a prince as he?
Where the nation live so free,
And so merry as do we?
Here at liberty we are,
And enjoy our ease and rest;
To the field we are not pressed;
Nor are called into the town
To be troubled with the gown.
Hang all officers, we cry,
And the magistrate too, by.
When the subsidy's increased,
We are not a penny cessed;
Nor will any go to law
With the beggar for a straw.
All which happiness, he brags,
He doth owe unto his rags.

John Fletcher (1579–1625)
A playwright whose fame, in his time, equalled that of his friend
and colleague William Shakespeare, Fletcher followed
Shakespeare as the leading writer for the theatre company known
as The King's Men.

THE MONTHS
by Sara Coleridge

January brings the snow,
Makes our feet and fingers glow.

February brings the rain,
Thaws the frozen lake again.

March brings breezes loud and shrill,
Stirs the dancing daffodil.

April brings the primrose sweet,
Scatters daisies at our feet.

May brings flocks of pretty lambs,
Skipping by their fleecy dams.

June brings tulips, lilies, roses,
Fills the children's hands with posies.

Hot July brings cooling showers,
Apricots and gillyflowers.

August brings the sheaves of corn,
Then the harvest home is borne.

Warm September brings the fruit,
Sportsmen then begin to shoot.

Fresh October brings the pheasant,
Then to gather nuts is pleasant.

Dull November brings the blast,
Then the leaves are whirling fast.

Chill December brings the sleet,
Blazing fire and holiday treat.

Sara Coleridge (1802–52)
The fourth child and only daughter of Samuel Taylor Coleridge,
Sara Coleridge was primarily an author and translator.
Coleridge was both her maiden name and her married name, as
she wed her cousin, Harry Nelson Coleridge.

THE WIND IN A FROLIC
by William Howitt

The wind one morning sprang up from sleep,
Saying, 'Now for a frolic! now for a leap!
Now for a madcap, galloping chase!
I'll make a commotion in every place!'
So it swept with a bustle right through a great town,
Creaking the signs, and scattering down
The shutters, and whisking, with merciless squalls,
Old women's bonnets and gingerbread stalls.
There never was heard a much lustier shout
As the apples and oranges tumbled about;
And urchins, that stand with their thievish eyes
Forever on watch, ran off each with a prize.

Then away to the fields it went blustering and humming,
And the cattle all wondered whatever was coming.
It plucked by their tails the grave matronly cows,
And tossed the colts' manes all about their brows,
Till offended at such a familiar salute,
They all turned their backs and stood silently mute.

So on it went, capering and playing its pranks;
Whistling with reeds on the broad river banks;
Puffing the birds, as they sat on a spray,
Or the travellers grave on the king's highway.
It was not too nice to bustle the bags
Of the beggar, and flutter his dirty rags.
'Twas so bold that it feared not to play its joke
With the doctor's wig, and the gentleman's cloak.
Through the forest it roared, and cried gayly, 'Now,
You sturdy old oaks, I'll make you bow!'
And it made them bow without more ado,
Or it cracked their great branches through and through.

Then it rushed like a monster o'er cottage and farm,
Striking their inmates with sudden alarm;
And they ran out like bees in a midsummer swarm.
There were dames with kerchiefs tied over their caps,
To see if their poultry were free from mishaps.
The turkeys they gobbled, the geese screamed aloud,
And the hens crept to roost in a terrified crowd;
There was rearing of ladders, and logs laying on,
Where the thatch from the roof threatened soon to be gone.
But the wind had passed on, and had met in a lane
With a schoolboy, who panted and struggled in vain,
For it tossed him, and twirled him, then passed, and he stood
With his hat in a pool and his shoe in the mud.

William Howitt (1792–1879)
_Born into a Quaker family in Derbyshire, William Howitt was the
author of over fifty books, some written in collaboration with his
wife Mary Howitt, the couple dedicating their efforts to providing
wholesome and instructive literature._

TO AUTUMN
by John Keats

Season of mists and mellow fruitfulness,
Close bosom-friend of the maturing sun;
Conspiring with him how to load and bless
With fruit the vines that round the thatch-eves run;
To bend with apples the moss'd cottage-trees,
And fill all fruit with ripeness to the core;
To swell the gourd, and plump the hazel shells
With a sweet kernel; to set budding more,
And still more, later flowers for the bees,
Until they think warm days will never cease,
For Summer has o'er-brimm'd their clammy cells.

Who hath not seen thee oft amid thy store?
Sometimes whoever seeks abroad may find
Thee sitting careless on a granary floor,
Thy hair soft-lifted by the winnowing wind;
Or on a half-reap'd furrow sound asleep,
Drows'd with the fume of poppies, while thy hook
Spares the next swath and all its twined flowers;
And sometimes like a gleaner thou dost keep
Steady thy laden head across a brook;
Or by a cider-press, with patient look,
Thou watchest the last oozings hours by hours.

Where are the songs of Spring? Ay, where are they.
  Think not of them, thou hast thy music too, –
  While barred clouds bloom the soft-dying day,
  And touch the stubble plains with rosy hue;
Then in a wailful choir the small gnats mourn
  Among the river sallows, borne aloft
  Or sinking as the light wind lives or dies;
And full-grown lambs loud bleat from hilly bourn;
  Hedge-crickets sing; and now with treble soft
  The red-breast whistles from a garden-croft;
  And gathering swallows twitter in the skies.

John Keats (1795–1821)
Despite dying of tuberculosis at the age of twenty-five, Keats left
behind a huge amount of verse including some epic masterpieces.
When he died, his last request was followed, and he was buried
under a tombstone reading, 'Here lies one whose name was writ
in water'. His name does not appear on the stone.

TREES
by Joyce Kilmer

I think that I shall never see
A poem lovely as a tree.

A tree whose hungry mouth is pressed
Against the earth's sweet flowing breast;

A tree that looks at God all day,
And lifts her leafy arms to pray;

A tree that may in summer wear
A nest of robins in her hair;

Upon whose bosom snow has lain;
Who intimately lives with rain.

Poems are made by fools like me,
But only God can make a tree.

Joyce Kilmer (1886–1918)
American journalist, poet and lexicographer, Alfred Joyce Kilmer
was inspired by nature and religion in much of his work, but
never with such success as the simple verse 'Trees' published in
1913. Sadly, when the United States entered the war against
Germany, Kilmer enlisted in the 69th Volunteer Infantry
Regiment and was killed at the Second Battle of Marne in 1918
at the age of thirty-one. A curious fact is that his father was the
man who invented Johnson's baby powder.

THE PEDLAR'S CARAVAN
by William Brighty Rands

I wish I lived in a caravan,
With a horse to drive, like the pedlarman!
Where he comes from nobody knows,
Nor where he goes to, but on he goes.

His caravan has windows two,
With a chimney of tin that the smoke comes through,
He has a wife, and a baby brown,
And they go riding from town to town.

'Chairs to mend and delf to sell!'
He clashes the basins like a bell.
Tea-trays, baskets, ranged in order,
Plates, with the alphabet round the border.

The roads are brown, and the sea is green,
But his house is just like a bathing-machine.
The world is round, but he can ride,
Rumble, and splash to the other side.

With the pedlarman I should like to roam,
And write a book when I come home.
All the people would read my book,
Just like the Travels of Captain Cook.

William Brighty Rands (1823–82)
Known as 'the laureate of the nursery', as well as writing some
very fine verse for children, Rands was the originator of the
Boy's Own Paper. *He also wrote a number of hymns and worked*
as a reporter in the committee rooms of the House of Commons.
'The Pedlar's Caravan' is one of the poems most often requested
by Daily Express *readers.*

THE VILLAGE BLACKSMITH
by Henry Wadsworth Longfellow

Under a spreading chestnut-tree
The village smithy stands;
The smith, a mighty man is he,
With large and sinewy hands;
And the muscles of his brawny arms
Are strong as iron bands.

His hair is crisp, and black, and long,
His face is like the tan;
His brow is wet with honest sweat,
He earns whate'er he can,
And looks the whole world in the face,
For he owes not any man.

Week in, week out, from morn till night,
You can hear his bellows blow;
You can hear him swing his heavy sledge,
With measured beat and slow,
Like a sexton ringing the village bell,
When the evening sun is low.

And children coming home from school
Look in at the open door;
They love to see the flaming forge,
And hear the bellows roar,
And catch the burning sparks that fly
Like chaff from a threshing-floor.

He goes on Sunday to the church,
And sits among his boys;
He hears the parson pray and preach,
He hears his daughter's voice,
Singing in the village choir,
And it makes his heart rejoice.

It sounds to him like her mother's voice,
Singing in Paradise!
He needs must think of her once more,
How in the grave she lies;
And with his hard, rough hand he wipes
A tear out of his eyes.

Toiling, – rejoicing, – sorrowing,
Onward through life he goes;
Each morning sees some task begin,
Each evening sees it close;
Something attempted, something done,
Has earned a night's repose.

Thanks, thanks to thee, my worthy friend,
For the lesson thou hast taught!
Thus at the flaming forge of life
Our fortunes must be wrought;
Thus on its sounding anvil shaped
Each burning deed and thought.

*This is one of Longfellow's most famous poems, written in 1841
and published in a collection entitled* Ballads And Other Poems.

MEG MERRILIES
by John Keats

Old Meg she was a gypsy;
And liv'd upon the moors:
Her bed it was the brown heath turf,
And her house was out of doors.

Her apples were swart blackberries,
Her currants, pods o' broom;
Her wine was dew of the wild white rose,
Her book a church-yard tomb.

Her brothers were the craggy hills,
Her sisters larchen trees;
Alone with her great family
She liv'd as she did please.

No breakfast had she many a morn,
No dinner many a noon,
And 'stead of supper she would stare
Full hard against the moon.

But every morn, of woodbine fresh
She made her garlanding,
And every night the dark glen yew
She wove, and she would sing.

And with her fingers old and brown
She plaited mats o' rushes,
And gave them to the cottagers
She met among the bushes.

Old Meg was brave as Margaret Queen,
And tall as Amazon:
An old red blanket cloak she wore,
A chip hat had she on.
God rest her aged bones somewhere –
She died full long agone!

*This poem is one of Keats' lighter works and was requested by
Jennifer Trodd of Havant who asked for it for her one-hundred-
year-old mother. 'She always loved "Meg she was a gypsy" and
could recite it off by heart'.*

THE MOON
by Robert Louis Stevenson

The moon has a face like the clock in the hall;
She shines on thieves on the garden wall,
On streets and fields and harbour quays,
And birdies asleep in the forks of the trees.
The squalling cat and the squeaking mouse,
The howling dog by the door of the house,
The bat that lies in bed at noon,
All love to be out by the light of the moon.
But all of the things that belong to the day,
Cuddle to sleep to be out of her way;
And flowers and children close their eyes
Till up in the morning the sun shall arise.

Carole Barlow of Blackpool wrote, 'When I was a young girl in the late 1940s, I remember receiving a book of poems for Christmas. The only one I really liked began "The moon has a face like the clock in the hall". I loved the poem but unfortunately cannot remember the rest.'

3.

Children's Verse

THE LAND OF COUNTERPANE
by Robert Louis Stevenson

When I was sick and lay a-bed,
I had two pillows at my head,
And all my toys beside me lay,
To keep me happy all the day.

And sometimes for an hour or so
I watched my leaden soldiers go,
With different uniforms and drills,
Among the bed-clothes, through the hills;

And sometimes sent my ships in fleets
All up and down among the sheets;
Or brought my trees and houses out,
And planted cities all about.

I was the giant great and still
That sits upon the pillow-hill,
And sees before him, dale and plain,
The pleasant land of counterpane.

This is a verse from Robert Louis Stevenson's Child's Garden of
Verses.

*Diana Steele from Wigan wrote, 'I remember from my
schooldays a poem that was something about a counterpane on a
child's bed. I hope you can help.'*

OVERHEARD ON A SALMARSH
by Harold Monro

Nymph, nymph, what are your beads?
Green glass, goblin. Why do you stare at them?
Give them me.
No.

Give them me. Give them me.
No.

Then I will howl all night in the reeds,
Lie in the mud and howl for them.

Goblin, why do you love them so?

They are better than stars or water,
Better than voices of winds that sing,
Better than any man's fair daughter,
Your green glass beads on a silver ring.

Hush, I stole them out of the moon.

Give me your beads, I want them.
No.

I will howl in the deep lagoon
For your green glass beads, I love them so.
Give them me. Give them.
No.

Harold Monro (1879–1932)
Harold Monro founded the journal Poetry Review *and started the Poetry Bookshop in London's Bloomsbury. He encouraged other poets by publishing and selling their works, and he also let several live in the rooms above the shop.*

THREE LITTLE KITTENS
from *Mother Goose*

Three little kittens they lost their mittens,
And they began to cry,
'Oh mother dear, we sadly fear
Our mittens we have lost.'
'What! Lost your mittens, you naughty kittens!
Then you shall have no pie.'
'Meeow, meeow, meeow,
Now we shall have no pie.'

The three little kittens they found their mittens,
And they began to cry,
'Oh mother dear, see here, see here
Our mittens we have found.'
'Put on your mittens, you silly kittens
And you shall have some pie.'
'Meeow, meeow, meeow,
Now let us have some pie.'

The three little kittens put on their mittens
And soon ate up the pie,
'Oh mother dear, we greatly fear
Our mittens we have soiled.'
'What! Soiled you mittens, you naughty kittens!'
Then they began to cry,
'Meeow, meeow, meeow.'
Then they began to sigh.

The three little kittens, they washed their mittens
And hung them out to dry,
'Oh mother dear, do you not hear
Our mittens we have washed.'
'What! washed your mittens, you are good kittens.'
But I smell a rat close by,
'Meeow, meeow, meeow.'
We smell a rat close by...

Mother Goose
*Nobody is quite sure where the original Mother Goose sprang
from, since she was already well known as a supposed teller of
children's stories long before the French writer Charles Perrault
published his first collection of Mother Goose stories in 1695.*

*Since then many other collections of nursery rhymes have
borne the Mother Goose label, but all seem to be traditional
rhymes of anonymous authorship.*

THE MOUSE AND THE CAKE
by Eliza Cook

A mouse found a beautiful piece of plum cake,
The richest and sweetest that mortal could make;
'Twas heavy with citron and fragrant with spice,
And covered in sugar all sparkling as ice.

'My stars!' cried the mouse, while his eyes beamed with glee,
'Here's a treasure I've found; what a feast it will be;
But hark! there's a noise, 'tis my brother at play;
So I'll hide with the cake lest they wander this way.

Not a bit shall they have, for I know I can eat
Every morsel myself, and I'll have such a treat.'
So off he went and held the cake fast,
While his hungry young brothers went scampering past.

He nibbled and nibbled, and panted, but still
He kept gulping it down till he made himself ill;
Yet he swallowed it all, and 'tis easy to guess,
He was soon so unwell that he groaned with distress.

His family heard him, and as he grew worse,
They sent for the doctor who made him rehearse
How he'd eaten the cake to the very last crumb,
Without giving his playmates and relatives some.

'Ah me!' cried the doctor, 'Advice is too late'
You must die before long, so prepare for your fate;
If you had but divided the cake with your brothers,
'Twould have done you no harm, and been good for the others.

Had you shared it, the treat had been wholesome enough,
But eaten by one, it was dangerous stuff;
So prepare for the worst, – and the word had scarce fled,
When the doctor turned round the patient was dead.

Now all little people the lesson may take,
And some large ones may learn from the mouse and the cake;
Not to be over selfish with what we may gain;
Or the best of our pleasures may yet turn to pain.

Eliza Cook (1818–89)
Eliza Cook was a successful Victorian writer whose down-to-earth verse made her especially popular among the working classes. She published the weekly Eliza Cook's Journal, *which she described as a publication of 'utility and amusement'. 'The Old Armchair', written in 1838, was the work that established her in the public imagination, but 'The Mouse and the Cake' became equally popular.*

FROM A RAILWAY CARRIAGE
by Robert Louis Stevenson

Faster than fairies, faster than witches,
Bridges and houses, hedges and ditches;
And charging along like troops in a battle,
All through the meadows, the horses and cattle:
All of the sights of the hill and the plain
Fly as thick as driving rain;
And ever again, in the wink of an eye,
Painted stations whistle by.

Here is a child who clambers and scrambles,
All by himself and gathering brambles;
Here is a tramp who stands and gazes;
And there is the green for stringing the daisies!
Here is a cart run away on the road
Lumping along with man and load;
And here is a mill and there is a river:
Each a glimpse and gone for ever!

A very popular poem, first requested by B Ellis, who remembered the first two lines from his schooldays in Yorkshire seventy years ago.

CHILD'S SONG IN SPRING
by Edith Nesbit

The Silver Birch is a dainty lady,
She wears a satin gown;
The elm tree makes the old churchyard shady,
She will not live in town.

The English oak is a sturdy fellow,
He gets his green coat late;
The willow is smart in a suit of yellow
While brown the beech trees wait.

Such a gay green gown God gives the larches –
As green as he is good!
The hazels hold up their arms for arches,
When spring rides through the wood.

The chestnut's proud, and the lilac's pretty,
The poplar's gentle and tall,
But the plane tree's kind to the poor dull city –
I love him best of all!

Edith Nesbit (1858–1924)
Writer or co-author of over sixty children's books, Edith Nesbit is best known for the ever-popular Railway Children. *She and her husband Hubert Bland were also among the founders of the Fabian Society, even underlining their socialist beliefs by naming their son Fabian.*

To judge from the number of requests we have had for this poem, it used to be very commonly taught in English schools, though few now remember more than the first couple of lines.

THE CHILDREN'S HOUR
by Henry Wadsworth Longfellow

Between the dark and the daylight,
When the night is beginning to lower,
Comes a pause in the day's occupations,
That is known as the Children's Hour.

I hear in the chamber above me
The patter of little feet,
The sound of a door that is opened,
And voices soft and sweet.

From my study I see in the lamplight,
Descending the broad hall stair,
Grave Alice, and laughing Allegra,
And Edith with golden hair.

A whisper, and then a silence:
Yet I know by their merry eyes
They are plotting and planning together
To take me by surprise.

A sudden rush from the stairway,
A sudden raid from the hall!
By three doors left unguarded
They enter my castle wall!

They climb up into my turret
O'er the arms and back of my chair;
If I try to escape, they surround me;
They seem to be everywhere.

They almost devour me with kisses,
  Their arms about me entwine,
Till I think of the Bishop of Bingen
  In his Mouse-Tower on the Rhine!

Do you think, o blue-eyed banditti,
  Because you have scaled the wall,
Such an old mustache as I am
  Is not a match for you all!

I have you fast in my fortress,
  And will not let you depart,
But put you down into the dungeon
  In the round-tower of my heart.

And there will I keep you forever,
  Yes, forever and a day,
Till the walls shall crumble to ruin,
  And moulder in dust away!

This poem was written by Longfellow in 1859, when his six children were aged between four and fifteen. It is a touching portrayal of the poet as a tender, loving father.

THE ELF AND THE DORMOUSE
by Oliver Herford

Under a Toadstool crept a wee Elf,
Out in the rain, to shelter himself.

Under the toadstool, sound asleep,
Sat a big Dormouse all in a heap.

Trembled the wee Elf, frightened, and yet
Fearing to fly away lest he get wet.

To the next shelter – maybe a mile!
Sudden the wee Elf smiled a wee smile,

Tugged till the toadstool toppled in two,
Holding it over him, gaily he flew.

Soon he was safe home, dry as could be,
Soon woke the Dormouse – 'Good gracious me!

Where is my toadstool?' loud he lamented.
And that's how umbrellas first were invented.

Oliver Herford (1863–1935)
A British-born American writer and illustrator, Herford's ready wit led to him being called 'the American Oscar Wilde'.
This poem was requested by Colin Pearson of Worcester, who wrote asking for a poem that, 'my mum read to me when I was a lad about sixty-four years ago' about a, 'wee elf who crept under a toadstool' which led to the invention of umbrellas.

4.

Our Country

THE GLORY OF THE GARDEN
by Rudyard Kipling

Our England is a garden that is full of stately views,
Of borders, beds and shrubberies and lawns and avenues,
With statues on the terraces and peacocks strutting by;
But the Glory of the Garden lies in more than meets the eye.

For where the old thick laurels grow, along the thin red wall,
You will find the tool- and potting-sheds which are the heart of all ;
The cold-frames and the hot-houses, the dungpits and the tanks:
The rollers, carts and drain-pipes, with the barrows and the planks.

And there you'll see the gardeners, the men and 'prentice boys
Told off to do as they are bid and do it without noise;
For, except when seeds are planted and we shout to scare the birds,
The Glory of the Garden it abideth not in words.

And some can pot begonias and some can bud a rose,
And some are hardly fit to trust with anything that grows;
But they can roll and trim the lawns and sift the sand and loam,
For the Glory of the Garden occupieth all who come.

Our England is a garden, and such gardens are not made
By singing: 'Oh, how beautiful!' and sitting in the shade,
While better men than we go out and start their working lives
At grubbing weeds from gravel-paths with broken dinner-knives

There's not a pair of legs so thin, there's not a head so thick,
There's not a hand so weak and white, nor yet a heart so sick.
But it can find some needful job that's crying to be done,
For the Glory of the Garden glorifieth every one.

Then seek your job with thankfulness and work till further orders,
If it's only netting strawberries or killing slugs on borders;
And when your back stops aching and your hands begin to harden,
You will find yourself a partner in the Glory of the Garden.

Oh, Adam was a gardener, and God who made him sees
That half a proper gardener's work is done upon his knees,
So when your work is finished, you can wash your hands and pray
For the Glory of the Garden, that it may not pass away!
And the Glory of the Garden it shall never pass away!

First published in 1911 in A School History of England *by
Kipling and Fletcher, this poem takes as its theme the view of a
nation as a garden, with its accompanying growth, development,
change and decay, and the work and commitment needed to keep
it in order.*

MY HEART'S IN THE HIGHLANDS
by Robert Burns

My heart's in the Highlands, my heart is not here,
My heart's in the Highlands a-chasing the deer –
A-chasing the wild deer, and following the roe;
My heart's in the Highlands, wherever I go.

Farewell to the Highlands, farewell to the North
The birth place of Valour, the country of Worth;
Wherever I wander, wherever I rove,
The hills of the Highlands for ever I love.

Farewell to the mountains high cover'd with snow;
Farewell to the straths and green valleys below;
Farewell to the forests and wild-hanging woods;
Farewell to the torrents and loud-pouring floods.

My heart's in the Highlands, my heart is not here,
My heart's in the Highlands a-chasing the deer –
Chasing the wild deer, and following the roe;
My heart's in the Highlands, wherever I go.

Robert Burns (1759–96)
Revered throughout the world as Scotland's unofficial national
poet, Burns produced a large body of work, mainly in a light
Scottish dialect that both preserved traditions and brought them
to a wider audience. His famous ode 'To A Haggis' is
ceremoniously read as the dish is served on Burns Night, the
anniversary of his birth on January 25.

HOME THOUGHTS FROM ABROAD
by Robert Browning

Oh, to be in England
Now that April's there,
And whoever wakes in England
Sees, some morning, unaware,
That the lowest boughs and the brushwood sheaf
Round the elm-tree bole are in tiny leaf,
While the chaffinch sings on the orchard bough
In England – now!

And after April, when May follows,
And the whitethroat builds, and all the swallows!
Hark, where my blossomed pear-tree in the hedge
Leans to the field and scatters on the clover
Blossoms and dewdrops – at the bent spray's edge –
That's the wise thrush; he sings each song twice over,
Lest you should think he never could recapture
The first fine careless rapture!
And though the fields look rough with hoary dew,
All will be gay when noontide wakes anew
The buttercups, the little children's dower –
Far brighter than this gaudy melon-flower!

Often misquoted as 'Oh to be in England, now that April's here,' remember this is Home Thoughts from Abroad. *It's about missing England, not enjoying it.*

THE RIVER'S TALE
by Rudyard Kipling

Twenty bridges from Tower to Kew
Wanted to know what the River knew,
Twenty Bridges or twenty-two,
For they were young, and the Thames was old
And this is the tale that River told:-

'I walk my beat before London Town,
Five hours up and seven down.
Up I go till I end my run
At Tide-end-town, which is Teddington.
Down I come with the mud in my hands
And plaster it over the Maplin Sands.
But I'd have you know that these waters of mine
Were once a branch of the River Rhine,
When hundreds of miles to the East I went
And England was joined to the Continent.

'I remember the bat-winged lizard-birds,
The Age of Ice and the mammoth herds,
And the giant tigers that stalked them down
Through Regent's Park into Camden Town.
And I remember like yesterday
The earliest Cockney who came my way,
When he pushed through the forest that lined the Strand,
With paint on his face and a club in his hand.
He was death to feather and fin and fur.
He trapped my beavers at Westminster.
He netted my salmon, he hunted my deer,
He killed my heron off Lambeth Pier.

He fought his neighbour with axes and swords,
Flint or bronze, at my upper fords,
While down at Greenwich, for slaves and tin,
The tall Phoenician ships stole in,

And North Sea war-boats, painted and gay,
Flashed like dragon-flies, Erith way;
And Norseman and Negro and Gaul and Greek
Drank with the Britons in Barking Creek,
And life was gay, and the world was new,
And I was a mile across at Kew!
But the Roman came with a heavy hand,
And bridged and roaded and ruled the land,
And the Roman left and the Danes blew in –
And that's where your history-books begin!'

*Requested by several readers, none of whom demanded a recount
on Kipling's bridge numbers. Neither now, nor in Kipling's time,
were there twenty, or even twenty-two, bridges across the
Thames. The deliberate vagueness emphasises that the precise
number of bridges is unimportant compared to the long history of
the River itself.*

INNOMINATUS
by Sir Walter Scott

Breathes there the man with soul so dead,
Who never to himself hath said,
'This is my own, my native land!'
Whose heart hath ne'er within him burn'd
As home his footsteps he hath turn'd
From wandering on a foreign strand?
If such there breathe, go, mark him well;
For him no Minstrel raptures swell;
High though his titles, proud his name,
Boundless his wealth as wish can claim;
Despite those titles, power, and pelf,
The wretch, concentred all in self,
Living, shall forfeit fair renown,
And, doubly dying, shall go down
To the vile dust from whence he sprung,
Unwept, unhonour'd, and unsung.

Sir Walter Scott (1771–1832)
Author of such classic novels as Ivanhoe *and* Rob Roy, *Sir Walter Scott was equally adept at producing epic tales in verse such as 'The Lay of the Last Minstrel' and 'Marmion'. His great influence on Scottish culture is marked by the impressive Scott Monument in Edinburgh.*

5.

All at Sea

CASABIANCA
by Felicia Dorothea Hemans

The boy stood on the burning deck
        Whence all but him had fled;
The flame that lit the battle's wreck
        Shone round him o'er the dead.

Yet beautiful and bright he stood,
        As born to rule the storm;
        A creature of heroic blood,
        A proud, though childlike form.

The flames rolled on – he would not go
        Without his father's word;
        That father, faint in death below,
        His voice no longer heard.

He called aloud – 'Say, father, say,
        If yet my task is done?'
He knew not that the chieftain lay
        Unconscious of his son.

'Speak, father!' once again he cried,
        'If I may yet be gone!'
And but the booming shots replied,
        And fast the flames rolled on.

Upon his brow he felt their breath,
        And in his waving hair,
And looked from that lone post of death
        In still, yet brave despair.

And shouted but once more aloud,
'My father! must I stay?'
While o'er him fast, through sail and shroud,
The wreathing fires made way.

They wrapt the ship in splendour wild,
They caught the flag on high,
And streamed above the gallant child,
Like banners in the sky.

There came a burst of thunder sound –
The boy – oh! where was he?
Ask of the winds that far around
With fragments strewed the sea! –

With mast, and helm, and pennon fair
That well had borne their part –
But the noblest thing that perished there
Was that young, faithful heart.

This poem tells of an incident during the Battle of the Nile when Casabianca, a boy aged about thirteen, son of the admiral of the Orient, remained at his post on the burning ship after all the guns had been abandoned. He died in the explosion when the flames reached the powder.

BIG STEAMERS
by Rudyard Kipling

Oh, where are you going to, all you Big Steamers,
With England's own coal, up and down the salt seas?
'We are going to fetch you your bread and your butter,
Your beef, pork, and mutton, eggs, apples, and cheese.'

'And where will you fetch it from, all you Big Steamers,
And where shall I write you when you are away?'
'We fetch it from Melbourne, Quebec, and Vancouver –
Address us at Hobart, Hong Kong, and Bombay.'

'But if anything happened to all you Big Steamers,
And suppose you were wrecked up and down the salt sea?'
'Why, you'd have no coffee or bacon for breakfast,
And you'd have no muffins or toast for your tea.'

'Then I'll pray for fine weather for all you Big Steamers
For little blue billows and breezes so soft.'
'Oh, billows and breezes don't bother Big Steamers:
We're iron below and steel-rigging aloft.'

'Then I'll build a new lighthouse for all you Big Steamers,
With plenty wise pilots to pilot you through.'
'Oh, the Channel's as bright as a ball-room already,
And pilots are thicker than pilchards at Looe.'

'Then what can I do for you, all you Big Steamers,
Oh, what can I do for your comfort and good?'
'Send out your big warships to watch your big waters,
That no one may stop us from bringing you food.'

'For the bread that you eat and the biscuits you nibble,
The sweets that you suck and the joints that you carve,
They are brought to you daily by all us Big Steamers –
And if any one hinders our coming you'll starve!'

This is one of Kipling's most popular verses, requested by many and remembered only vaguely from long-off schooldays.

DAYBREAK
by Henry Wadsworth Longfellow

A wind came up out of the sea,
And said, O mists, make room for me.

It hailed the ships, and cried, Sail on,
Ye mariners, the night is gone.

And hurried landward far away,
Crying, Awake! it is the day.

It said unto the forest, Shout!
Hang all your leafy banners out!

It touched the wood-bird's folded wing,
And said, O bird, awake and sing.

And o'er the farms, O chanticleer,
Your clarion blow; the day is near.

It whispered to the fields of corn,
Bow down, and hail the coming morn.

It shouted through the belfry-tower,
Awake, O bell! proclaim the hour.

It crossed the churchyard with a sigh,
And said, Not yet! in quiet lie.

---

*This poem was requested by Mrs Sybil Ainley, of Norwich. 'I
remember the first few lines of a poem I learned in 1927 or 1928,
beginning: "A wind came up out of the sea", but I cannot
continue it and have never come across it again.'*

BREAK, BREAK, BREAK
by Alfred, Lord Tennyson

Break, break, break,
On thy cold gray stones, O Sea!
And I would that my tongue could utter
The thoughts that arise in me.

O well for the fisherman's boy,
That he shouts with his sister at play!
O well for the sailor lad,
That he sings in his boat on the bay!

And the stately ships go on
To their haven under the hill;
But O for the touch of a vanish'd hand,
And the sound of a voice that is still!

Break, break, break
At the foot of thy crags, O Sea!
But the tender grace of a day that is dead
Will never come back to me.

This is wonderful evocation of the rhythms and moods of the sea.
The poem was requested by Janet Cutts of Reading, who wrote,
'Many years ago, I used to read poetry when working on the ship
Transvaal Castle. *Can you complete the poem with the lines "Oh*
for the touch of a vanished hand, And the sound of a voice that is
gone"?'

THE THREE FISHERS
by Charles Kingsley

Three fishers went sailing away to the west,
　　Away to the west as the sun went down;
Each thought on the woman who loved him the best,
And the children stood watching them out of the town;
　　For men must work, and women must weep,
　　And there's little to earn, and many to keep,
　　　Though the harbour bar be moaning.

Three wives sat up in the lighthouse tower,
　　And they trimmed the lamps as the sun went down;
They looked at the squall, and they looked at the shower,
And the night-rack came rolling up ragged and brown.
　　But men must work, and women must weep,
　　Though storms be sudden, and waters deep,
　　　And the harbour bar be moaning.

Three corpses lay out on the shining sands
　　In the morning gleam as the tide went down,
And the women are weeping and wringing their hands
For those who will never come home to the town;
　　For men must work, and women must weep,
　　And the sooner it's over, the sooner to sleep;
　　　And good-bye to the bar and its moaning.

This poem was requested by Mrs Jeanie Kerr. 'I can't remember much of it, but the bit that sticks in my mind is "For men must work and women must weep, there's little to earn and much to keep." I think it's called Harbour Bar Be Moaning.'

6.

Affairs of the Heart

EDWARD GRAY
by Alfred, Lord Tennyson

Sweet Emma Moreland of yonder town
    Met me walking on yonder way;
'And have you lost your heart?' she said;
'And are you married yet, Edward Gray?'

Sweet Emma Moreland spoke to me;
    Bitterly weeping I turn'd away:
'Sweet Emma Moreland, love no more
Can touch the heart of Edward Gray.

'Ellen Adair she loved me well,
Against her father's and mother's will;
    To-day I sat for an hour and wept
By Ellen's grave, on the windy hill.

'Shy she was, and I thought her cold,
Thought her proud, and fled over the sea;
    Fill'd I was with folly and spite,
When Ellen Adair was dying for me.

'Cruel, cruel the words I said!
    Cruelly came they back to-day:
"You're too slight and fickle," I said,
"To trouble the heart of Edward Gray."

'There I put my face in the grass –
    Whisper'd, "Listen to my despair;
I repent me of all I did;
    Speak a little, Ellen Adair!"

'Then I took a pencil, and wrote
On the mossy stone, as I lay,
"Here lies the body of Ellen Adair;
And here the heart of Edward Gray!"

'Love may come, and love may go,
And fly, like a bird, from tree to tree;
But I will love no more, no more,
Till Ellen Adair come back to me.

'Bitterly wept I over the stone;
Bitterly weeping I turn'd away.
There lies the body of Ellen Adair!
And there the heart of Edward Gray!'

'I always feel so sorry for Ellen Adair,' Noma Potter wrote. 'This was a poem I loved over fifty years ago, but now I can only recall a line here and there: "Ellen Adair, she loved me well, Against her father's and mother's will". I would love to know the full poem.'

SALLY IN OUR ALLEY
by Henry Carey

Of all the girls that are so smart
There's none like pretty Sally;
She is the darling of my heart,
And she lives in our alley.
There is no lady in the land
Is half so sweet as Sally;
She is the darling of my heart,
And she lives in our alley.

Her father he makes cabbage-nets,
And through the streets does cry 'em;
Her mother she sells laces long
To such as please to buy 'em;
But sure such folks could ne'er beget
So sweet a girl as Sally!
She is the darling of my heart,
And she lives in our alley.

When she is by, I leave my work,
I love her so sincerely;
My master comes like any Turk,
And bangs me most severely:
But let him bang his bellyful,
I'll bear it all for Sally;
She is the darling of my heart,
And she lives in our alley.

Of all the days that's in the week
I dearly love but one day –
And that's the day that comes betwixt
A Saturday and Monday;
For then I'm drest all in my best

To walk abroad with Sally;
She is the darling of my heart,
And she lives in our alley.

My master carries me to church,
And often am I blamed
Because I leave him in the lurch
As soon as text is named;
I leave the church in sermon-time
And slink away to Sally;
She is the darling of my heart,
And she lives in our alley.

When Christmas comes about again,
O, then I shall have money;
I'll hoard it up, and box it all,
I'll give it to my honey:
I would it were ten thousand pound,
I'd give it all to Sally;
She is the darling of my heart,
And she lives in our alley.

My master and the neighbours all
Make game of me and Sally,
And, but for her, I'd better be
A slave and row a galley;
But when my seven long years are out,
O, then I'll marry Sally;
O, then we'll wed, and then we'll bed –
But not in our alley!

Henry Carey (c. 1693–1743)
This verse was first published in 1726 in a collection of works by Henry Carey the English composer and playwright.

ANSWERED
by Ella Wheeler Wilcox

Good-bye – Yes, I am going.
Sudden? Well, you are right.
But a startling truth came home to me
With sudden force last night.

What is it? Shall I tell you –
Nay, that is why I go.
I am running away from the battlefield,
Turning my back on the foe.

Riddles? You think me cruel!
Have you not been most kind?
Why, when you question me like that
What answer can I find?

You fear you failed to amuse me,
Your husband's friend and guest,
Whom he bade you entertain and please –
Well, you have done your best.

Then why, you ask, am I going?
A friend of mine abroad,
Whose theories I have been acting upon,
Has proven himself a fraud.

You have heard me quote from Plato
A thousand times no doubt;
Well, I have discovered he did not know
What he was talking about.

You think I am speaking strangely?
You cannot understand?
Well, let me look down into your eyes,
And let me take your hand.

I am running away from danger –
I am flying before I fall;
I am going because with heart and soul
I love you – that is all.

There, now, you are white with anger,
I knew it would be so.
You should not question a man too close
When he tells you he must go.

Ella Wheeler Wilcox (1850–1919)
Good cheer and optimism are the themes of many works by the
American poet Ella Wheeler Wilcox. Her philosophy is perhaps
best summed up in the opening lines of 'The Man Worth While':
'It is easy enough to be pleasant, When life flows by like a song,
But the man worth while is one who will smile, When everything
goes dead wrong.'

LOCHINVAR
by Sir Walter Scott

Oh! young Lochinvar is come out of the west,
Through the wide Border his steed was the best;
And save his good broadsword he weapons had none.
He rode all unarmed and he rode all alone.
So faithful in love and so dauntless in war,
There never was knight like the young Lochinvar.

He stayed not for brake and he stopped not for stone,
He swam the Eske river where ford there was none,
But ere he alighted at Netherby gate
The bride had consented, the gallant came late:
For a laggard in love and a dastard in war
Was to wed the fair Ellen of brave Lochinvar.

So boldly he entered the Netherby Hall,
Among bridesmen, and kinsmen, and brothers, and all:
Then spoke the bride's father, his hand on his sword, –
For the poor craven bridegroom said never a word, –
'Oh! come ye in peace here, or come ye in war,
Or to dance at our bridal, young Lord Lochinvar?' –

'I long wooed your daughter, my suit you denied;
Love swells like the Solway, but ebbs like its tide –
And now am I come, with this lost love of mine,
To lead but one measure, drink one cup of wine,
There are maidens in Scotland more lovely by far,
That would gladly be bride to the young Lochinvar.

The bride kissed the goblet; the knight took it up,
He quaffed off the wine, and he threw down the cup.
She looked down to blush, and she looked up to sigh,
WIth a smile on her lips and a tear in her eye.
He took her soft hand ere her mother could bar, –
'Now tread we a measure!' said young Lochinvar.

So stately his form, and so lovely her face,
That never a hall such a galliard did grace;
While her mother did fret, and her father did fume,
And the bridegroom stood dangling his bonnet and plume;
And the bride-maidens whispered, ''Twere better by far
To have matched our fair cousin with young Lochinvar.'

One touch to her hand and one word in her ear,
When they reached the hall-door, and the charger stood near;
So light to the croupe the fair lady he swung,
So light to the saddle before her he sprung!
'She is won! we are gone, over bank, bush and scaur;
They'll have fleet steeds that follow,' quoth young Lochinvar.

There was mounting 'mong Graemes of the Netherby clan;
Forsters, Fenwicks, and Musgraves, they rode and they ran!
There was racing and chasing on Cannobie Lee,
But the lost bride of Netherby ne'er did they see.
So daring in love and so dauntless in war,
Have ye e'er heard of gallant like young Lochinvar?

Sir Walter Scott (1771–1832)
One of the often requested poems that is too long for the
Forgotten Verse slot in the Daily Express, *'Lochinvar' is in fact*
only a small part of an even longer work.
Sir Walter Scott wrote a number of long ballads – about the
days of chivalry, of outlaws and of the culture of the Scottish
Border region – included in his epic verse called 'Marmion'.

SOMEBODY'S DARLING
by Marie Ravenel de la Coste

Into a ward of the whitewashed halls,
Where the dead and dying lay,
Wounded by bayonets, shells, and balls,
Somebody's darling was borne one day;

Somebody's darling, so young and brave,
Wearing yet on his pale, sweet face,
Soon to be hid by the dust of the grave,
The lingering light of his boyhood's grace.

Matted and damp are the curls of gold,
Kissing the snow of that fair young brow;
Pale are the lips of delicate mold
Somebody's darling is dying now.

Back from his beautiful, blue-veined brow,
Brush all the wandering waves of gold;
Cross his hands, on his bosom now;
Somebody's darling is still and cold.

Kiss him once for somebody's sake,
Murmur a prayer soft and low;
One bright curl from its fair mates take;
They were somebody's pride, you know;

Somebody's hand has rested there;
Was it a mother's, soft and white?
And have the lips of a sister fair
Been baptized in the waves of light?

God knows best! He was somebody's love.
Somebody's heart enshrined him there;
Somebody wafted his name above,
Night and morn, on the wings of prayer.

Somebody wept when he marched away,
Looking so handsome, brave, and grand;
Somebody's kiss on his forehead lay;
Somebody clung to his parting hand.

Somebody's watching and waiting for him,
Yearning to hold him again to her heart;
And there he lies, with his blue eyes dim,
And the smiling, childlike lips apart.

Tenderly bury the fair young dead,
Pausing to drop on his grave a tear;
Carve on the wooden slab at his head,
'Somebody's darling slumbers here.'

Marie Ravenel de la Coste (?–1936)
Marie Ravenel de la Coste was the daughter of French parents
who had emigrated to Savannah, Georgia. She worked as a
French teacher, but began to write poetry when her fiance, a
captain in the Confederate Army, was killed in battle. After his
death, Marie often visited wounded soldiers in Savannah's
hospitals, bringing them flowers and fruit and keeping them
company.

RUTH
by Thomas Hood

She stood breast-high amid the corn,
Clasp'd by the golden light of morn,
    Like the sweetheart of the sun,
Who many a glowing kiss had won.

On her cheek an autumn flush,
Deeply ripen'd; – such a blush
    In the midst of brown was born,
Like red poppies grown with corn.

Round her eyes her tresses fell,
Which were blackest none could tell,
    But long lashes veil'd a light,
That had else been all too bright.

And her hat, with shady brim,
Made her tressy forehead dim;
    Thus she stood amid the stooks,
Praising God with sweetest looks:–

Sure, I said, Heav'n did not mean,
Where I reap thou shouldst but glean,
    Lay thy sheaf adown and come,
Share my harvest and my home.

Thomas Hood (1799–1845)
*This poem was requested, appropriately enough, in an e-mail
from Ruth Abbey, looking for her own name: 'I have searched for
the poem Ruth "there she stood amid the corn". Can you help
please?'*

7.

War

THE CHARGE OF THE LIGHT BRIGADE
by Alfred, Lord Tennyson

Half a league, half a league,
Half a league onward,
All in the valley of Death
Rode the six hundred.
'Forward, the Light Brigade!
Charge for the guns!' he said:
Into the valley of Death
Rode the six hundred.

'Forward, the Light Brigade!'
Was there a man dismay'd ?
Not tho' the soldier knew
Some one had blunder'd:
Theirs not to make reply,
Theirs not to reason why,
Theirs but to do and die,
Into the valley of Death
Rode the six hundred.

Cannon to right of them,
Cannon to left of them,
Cannon in front of them
Volley'd & thunder'd;
Storm'd at with shot and shell,
Boldly they rode and well,
Into the jaws of Death,
Into the mouth of Hell
Rode the six hundred.

Flash'd all their sabres bare,
Flash'd as they turn'd in air
Sabring the gunners there,
Charging an army, while
All the world wonder'd:
Plunged in the battery-smoke
Right thro' the line they broke;
Cossack and Russian
Reel'd from the sabre-stroke,
Shatter'd and sunder'd.
Then they rode back, but not
Not the six hundred.

Cannon to right of them,
Cannon to left of them,
Cannon behind them
Volley'd and thunder'd;
Storm'd at with shot and shell,
While horse and hero fell,
They that had fought so well
Came thro' the jaws of Death,
Back from the mouth of Hell,
All that was left of them,
Left of six hundred.

When can their glory fade?
O the wild charge they made!
All the world wonder'd.
Honour the charge they made!
Honour the Light Brigade,
Noble six hundred!

Tennyson wrote this poem only minutes after reading an account of the battle of Balaclava in The Times.

HOME THEY BROUGHT HER WARRIOR DEAD
by Alfred, Lord Tennyson

Home they brought her warrior dead:
She nor swooned, nor uttered cry:
All her maidens, watching, said,
'She must weep or she will die.'

Then they praised him, soft and low,
Called him worthy to be loved,
Truest friend and noblest foe;
Yet she neither spoke nor moved.

Stole a maiden from her place,
Lightly to the warrior stepped,
Took the face-cloth from the face;
Yet she neither moved nor wept.

Rose a nurse of ninety years,
Set his child upon her knee –
Like summer tempest came her tears –
'Sweet my child, I live for thee.'

*This was requested by Vijay Sawant, who learned the poem while
studying English as a foreign language in India.*

IN FLANDERS FIELDS
by John McCrae

In Flanders Fields the poppies blow
Between the crosses row on row,
That mark our place; and in the sky
The larks, still bravely singing, fly
Scarce heard amid the guns below.

We are the Dead. Short days ago
We lived, felt dawn, saw sunset glow,
Loved and were loved, and now we lie
In Flanders fields.

Take up our quarrel with the foe:
To you from failing hands we throw
The torch; be yours to hold it high.
If ye break faith with us who die
We shall not sleep, though poppies grow
In Flanders fields.

John McCrae (1872–1918)
The author of one of the most poignant of all First World War
poems, McCrae was a doctor appointed as a field surgeon in the
Canadian Artillery and was in charge of a field hospital during
the Second Battle of Ypres in 1915. His friend and former
student, Lt. Alexis Helmer, was killed in the battle, and his burial
inspired the poem, which was written on 3 May 1915. After
showing it to a colleague, McCrae tossed the poem away, but
another officer retrieved it and sent it to newspapers in England.
It was published in December 1915.

THE BURIAL OF SIR JOHN MOORE
AT CORUNNA
by Charles Wolfe

Not a drum was heard, nor a funeral note,
As his corpse to the rampart we hurried;
Not a soldier discharged his farewell shot
O'er the grave where our hero we buried.

We buried him darkly at dead of night,
The sods with our bayonets turning;
By the struggling moonbeam's misty light
And the lantern dimly burning.

No useless coffin enclosed his breast,
Nor in sheet nor in shroud we wound him;
But he lay like a warrior taking his rest
With his martial cloak around him.

Few and short were the prayers we said,
And we spoke not a word of sorrow;
But we steadfastly gazed on the face that was dead,
And we bitterly thought of the morrow.

We thought, as we hollowed his narrow bed
And smoothed down his lonely pillow,
That the foe and the stranger would tread o'er his head,
And we far away on the billow!

Lightly they'll talk of the spirit that's gone
And o'er his cold ashes upbraid him, –
But little he'll reck, if they let him sleep on
In the grave where a Briton has laid him.

But half of our heavy task was done
When the clock struck the hour for retiring:
And we heard the distant and random gun
That the foe was sullenly firing.

Slowly and sadly we laid him down,
From the field of his fame fresh and gory;
We carved not a line, and we raised not a stone,
But left him alone with his glory.

Charles Wolfe (1791–1823)
*Scarcely known outside Dublin even in his own lifetime, the Irish
poet Charles Wolfe is now remembered almost solely for this one
stirring poem. He was ordained a priest in 1817 and became
curate of Ballyclog in County Tyrone.*

INCIDENT OF THE FRENCH CAMP
by Robert Browning

You know, we French stormed Ratisbon:
    A mile or so away,
On a little mound, Napoleon
    Stood on our storming-day;
With neck out-thrust, you fancy how,
    Legs wide, arms locked behind,
As if to balance the prone brow
    Oppressive with its mind.

Just as perhaps he mused, 'My plans
    That soar, to earth may fall,
Let once my army-leader Lannes
    Waver a yonder wall,' –
Out 'twixt the battery-smokes there flew
    A rider, bound on bound
Full-galloping; nor bridle drew
    Until he reached the mound.

Then off there flung in smiling joy,
    And held himself erect
By just his horse's mane, a boy:
    You hardly could suspect –
(So tight he kept his lips compressed,
    Scarce any blood came through)
You looked twice ere you saw his breast
    Was all but shot in two.

'Well,' cried he, 'Emperor, by God's grace
We've got you Ratisbon!
The Marshal's in the market-place,
And you'll be there anon
To see your flag-bird flap his vans
Where I, to heart's desire,
Perched him!' The chief's eye flashed; his plans
Soared up again like fire.

The chief's eye flashed; but presently
Softened itself, as sheathes
A film the mother-eagle's eye
When her bruised eaglet breathes:
'You're wounded!' 'Nay', the soldier's pride
Touched to quick, he said:
'I'm killed, Sire!' And his chief beside,
Smiling the boy fell dead.

*The poem is set at the The Battle of Ratisbon (or Regensburg) in
1809 between France and Austria. During the battle Napoleon
himself was wounded by a bullet, which hit his ankle. He was not
seriously hurt by the shot, which had been fired from a great
distance, but it was the only time in all his campaigns that
Napoleon was wounded.*

THE SOLDIER
by Rupert Brooke

If I should die, think only this of me:
That there's some corner of a foreign field
That is for ever England. There shall be
In that rich earth a richer dust concealed;
A dust whom England bore, shaped, made aware,
Gave, once, her flowers to love, her ways to roam,
A body of England's, breathing English air,
Washed by the rivers, blest by suns of home.
And think, this heart, all evil shed away,
A pulse in the eternal mind, no less
Gives somewhere back the thoughts by England given;
Her sights and sounds; dreams happy as her day;
And laughter, learnt of friends; and gentleness,
In hearts at peace, under an English heaven.

This poem was requested by Jessie Slater, whose comments perfectly express the appeal of Forgotten Verse: 'In 1929, I left school aged fourteen. Some poems I learned at school I must have recited hundreds of times since then. Now I find I can only remember bits of them.'

8.

Faith and Devotion

SONNET 19
by John Milton

When I consider how my light is spent,
Ere half my days, in this dark world and wide,
And that one talent which is death to hide
Lodged with me useless, though my soul more bent
To serve therewith my Maker, and present
My true account, lest He returning chide,
'Doth God exact day-labour, light denied?'
I fondly ask. But patience, to prevent
That murmur, soon replies, 'God doth not need
Either man's work or his own gifts. Who best
Bear His mild yoke, they serve Him best. His state
Is kingly: thousands at His bidding speed
And post o'er land and ocean without rest;
They also serve who only stand and wait.'

John Milton (1608–74)
Milton's 'Paradise Lost' and the later 'Paradise Regained' are
justly seen as two of the great examples of English epic poetry.
The opening line of the verse above – often misquoted with 'life'
in place of 'light' – is a reference to the blindness with which
Milton was affllicted in later life.'

THE LAMB
by William Blake

Little Lamb, who made thee?
Dost thou know who made thee?
Gave thee life, and bid thee feed,
By the stream and o'er the mead;
Gave thee clothing of delight,
Softest clothing, woolly, bright;
Gave thee such a tender voice,
Making all the vales rejoice?
Little Lamb, who made thee?
Dost thou know who made thee?

Little Lamb, I'll tell thee,
Little Lamb, I'll tell thee.
He is called by thy name,
For He calls Himself a Lamb.
He is meek, and He is mild;
He became a little child.
I a child, and thou a lamb,
We are called by His name.
Little Lamb, God bless thee!
Little Lamb, God bless thee!

William Blake (1757–1827)
A visionary artist and poet, William Blake's creative, mystical, and often prophetic writings were so unconventional that he was considered mad by several of his contemporaries. His belief that he could converse with Old Testament prophets may have encouraged that view. William Wordsworth wrote of Blake: 'There was no doubt that this poor man was mad, but there is something in the madness of this man which interests me more than the sanity of Lord Byron and Walter Scott.'

ABOU BEN ADHEM
by James Henry Leigh Hunt

Abou Ben Adhem (may his tribe increase!)
Awoke one night from a deep dream of peace,
And saw – within the moonlight in his room,
Making it rich, and like a lily in bloom –
An Angel, writing in a book of gold:

Exceeding peace had made Ben Adhem bold,
And to the Presence in the room he said,
'What writest thou?' The Vision raised its head,
And with a look made of all sweet accord
Answered, 'The names of those who love the Lord.'

'And is mine one?' said Abou. 'Nay, not so,'
Replied the Angel. Abou spoke more low,
But cheerily still; and said, 'I pray thee, then,
Write me as one who loves his fellow men.'

The Angel wrote, and vanished. The next night
It came again with a great wakening light,
And showed the names whom love of God had blessed,
And, lo! Ben Adhem's name led all the rest!

James Henry Leigh Hunt (1784–1859)
*'Abou Ben Adhem' is one of the most frequently requested poems
by the* Daily Express *Forgotten Verse readers, with widely
varying spellings of the title.*

GOD'S GARDEN
by Dorothy Frances Gurney

The Lord God planted a garden
In the first white days of the world,
And He set there an angel warden
In a garment of light enfurled.

So near to the peace of Heaven,
That the hawk might nest with the wren,
For there in the cool of the even
God walked with the first of men.

And I dream that these garden-closes
With their shade and their sun-flecked sod
And their lilies and bowers of roses,
Were laid by the hand of God.

The kiss of the sun for pardon,
The song of the birds for mirth, –
One is nearer God's heart in a garden
Than anywhere else on earth.

For He broke it for us in a garden
Under the olive-trees
Where the angel of strength was the warden
And the soul of the world found ease.

Dorothy Frances Gurney (1858–1932)
*Dorothy Frances Gurney was a hymn-writer and poet whose
grandfather had been the Bishop of London.*

MY GARDEN
by Thomas Edward Brown

A garden is a lovesome thing, God wot!
Rose plot,
Fringed pool,
Ferned grot –
The veriest school
Of peace; and yet the fool
Contends that God is not –
Not God! in gardens! when the eve is cool?
Nay, but I have a sign;
'Tis very sure God walks in mine.

Thomas Edward Brown (1830–97)
*Born on the Isle of Man, Thomas Edward Brown was a brilliant
theologian and scholar, gaining a double first at Oxford and
becoming headmaster of the Crypt School in Gloucester, then a
senior master at Clifton College. The opening line of this verse
must be one of the best-known in English poetry, though few
know who wrote it.*

9.

Humorous Verse

THE WALRUS AND THE CARPENTER
by Lewis Carroll

The sun was shining on the sea,
　　Shining with all his might:
He did his very best to make
　　The billows smooth and bright –
And this was odd, because it was
　　The middle of the night.

The moon was shining sulkily,
　　Because she thought the sun
Had got no business to be there
　　After the day was done –
'It's very rude of him,' she said,
　　'To come and spoil the fun!'

The sea was wet as wet could be,
　　The sands were dry as dry.
You could not see a cloud, because
　　No cloud was in the sky:
No birds were flying overhead –
　　There were no birds to fly.

The Walrus and the Carpenter
　　Were walking close at hand;
They wept like anything to see
　　Such quantities of sand:
'If this were only cleared away,'
　　They said, 'it would be grand!'

'If seven maids with seven mops
Swept it for half a year.
Do you suppose,' the Walrus said,
'That they could get it clear?'
'I doubt it,' said the Carpenter,
And shed a bitter tear.

'O Oysters, come and walk with us!'
The Walrus did beseech.
'A pleasant walk, a pleasant talk,
Along the briny beach:
We cannot do with more than four,
To give a hand to each.'

The eldest Oyster looked at him,
But never a word he said:
The eldest Oyster winked his eye,
And shook his heavy head –
Meaning to say he did not choose
To leave the oyster-bed.

But four young Oysters hurried up,
All eager for the treat:
Their coats were brushed, their faces washed,
Their shoes were clean and neat –
And this was odd, because, you know,
They hadn't any feet.

Four other Oysters followed them,
And yet another four;
And thick and fast they came at last,
And more, and more, and more –
All hopping through the frothy waves,
And scrambling to the shore.

The Walrus and the Carpenter
Walked on a mile or so,
And then they rested on a rock
Conveniently low:
And all the little Oysters stood
And waited in a row.

'The time has come,' the Walrus said,
'To talk of many things:
Of shoes - and ships – and sealing-wax –
Of cabbages – and kings –
And why the sea is boiling hot –
And whether pigs have wings.'

'But wait a bit,' the Oysters cried,
'Before we have our chat;
For some of us are out of breath,
And all of us are fat!'
'No hurry!' said the Carpenter.
They thanked him much for that.

'A loaf of bread,' the Walrus said,
'Is what we chiefly need:
Pepper and vinegar besides
Are very good indeed –
Now if you're ready, Oysters dear,
We can begin to feed.'

'But not on us!' the Oysters cried,
Turning a little blue.
'After such kindness, that would be
A dismal thing to do!'
'The night is fine,' the Walrus said.
'Do you admire the view?

'It was so kind of you to come!
And you are very nice!'
The Carpenter said nothing but
'Cut us another slice:
I wish you were not quite so deaf –
I've had to ask you twice!'

'It seems a shame,' the Walrus said,
'To play them such a trick,
After we've brought them out so far,
And made them trot so quick!'
The Carpenter said nothing but
'The butter's spread too thick!'

'I weep for you,' the Walrus said:
'I deeply sympathize.'
With sobs and tears he sorted out
Those of the largest size,
Holding his pocket-handkerchief
Before his streaming eyes.

'O Oysters,' said the Carpenter,
'You've had a pleasant run!
Shall we be trotting home again?'
But answer came there none –
And this was scarcely odd, because
They'd eaten every one.

This poem comes from Through The Looking Glass, *where
Tweedledum and Tweedledee recite it to Alice. Whether it is a
piece of Carrollian whimsy, or a satire on the corruption of
politicians and the nature of genocide, is still a matter of dispute.
One interesting fact is that Carroll did not decide who the
Walrus's companion was. He told his illustrator, John Tenniel, to
choose whichever he liked from Carpenter, Butterfly and Baronet.*

A TRAGIC STORY
by William Makepeace Thackeray

There lived a sage in days of yore,
And he a handsome pigtail wore;
But wondered much, and sorrowed more,
Because it hung behind him.

He mused upon the curious case,
And swore he'd change the pigtail's place,
And have it hanging at his face,
Not dangling there behind him.

Says he, 'The mystery I've found, –
I'll turn me round,'– he turned him round;
But still it hung behind him.

Then round and round, and out and in,
All day the puzzled sage did spin;
In vain – it mattered not a pin, –
The pigtail hung behind him.

And right, and left, and round about,
And up, and down, and in, and out
He turned; but still the pigtail stout
Hung steadily behind him.

And though his efforts never slack,
And though he twist, and twirl, and tack,
Alas! still faithful to his back,
The pigtail hangs behind him.

William Makepeace Thackeray (1811–63)
Best known now for his satirical novel Vanity Fair, *Thackeray*
was ranked second only to Dickens as a novelist in Victorian
times. The above poem is a translation into verse of a work by
the German poet Adelbert von Chamisso (1781–1838).

THE IRISH PIG
Anonymous

'Twas an evening in November,
As I very well remember.
I was strolling down the street in drunken pride,
But my knees were all aflutter,
So I landed in the gutter,
And a pig came up and lay down by my side.
Yes, I lay there in the gutter
Thinking thoughts I could not utter,
When a colleen passing by did softly say,
'You can tell a man that boozes
By the company he chooses.'
At that the pig got up and walked away!

Requested by many and usually described as, 'the one where the pig gets up and walks away'. The verse was made popular in a 1933 song 'The Pig Got Up and Slowly Walked Away' by Benjamin Hapgood Burt, which began 'One evening in October, when I was one-third sober', but the original seems to be an older, anonymous poem called 'The Irish Pig'.

INCIDENTS IN THE LIFE OF MY UNCLE ARLY
by Edward Lear

O! My aged Uncle Arly!
Sitting on a heap of Barley
Thro' the silent hours of night, –
Close beside a leafy thicket: –
On his nose there was a Cricket, –
In his hat a Railway-Ticket; –
(But his shoes were far too tight.)

Long ago, in youth, he squander'd
All his goods away, and wander'd
To the Tiniskoop-hills afar.
There on golden sunsets blazing,
Every morning found him gazing, –
Singing – 'Orb! you're quite amazing!
How I wonder what you are!'

Like the ancient Medes and Persians,
Always by his own exertions
He subsisted on those hills; –
Whiles, – by teaching children spelling, –
Or at times by merely yelling, –
Or at intervals by selling
'Propter's Nicodemus Pills.'

Later, in his morning rambles
He perceived the moving brambles –
Something square and white disclose; –
'Twas a First-class Railway Ticket;
But, on stooping down to pick it
Off the ground, – a pea-green Cricket
settled on my uncle's Nose.

Never – never more, – Oh! never,
Did that Cricket leave him ever, –
Dawn or evening, day or night; –
Clinging as a constant treasure, –
Chirping with a cheerious measure, –
Wholly to my uncle's pleasure
(Though his shoes were far too tight.)

So for three-and-forty winters,
Till his shoes were worn to splinters,
All those hills he wander'd o'er, –
Sometimes silent; – sometimes yelling; –
Till he came to Borley-Melling,
Near his old ancestral dwelling; –
(But his shoes were far too tight.)

On a little heap of Barley
Died my aged uncle Arly,
And they buried him one night; –
Close beside the leafy thicket; –
There, – his hat and Railway-Ticket; –
There, – his ever-faithful Cricket; –
(But his shoes were far too tight.)

Edward Lear (1812–88)
*Pioneer of limericks and nonsense verse, Edward Lear has been
loved by generations for his humour and verbal inventiveness.
He wrote 'The Owl And The Pussy-Cat' for his patron, the Earl
of Derby.*

*This was requested by Julie Briggs of Shrewsbury. 'I wonder
if you could find a poem my late mother often recited to me. All I
can remember is the start: "O, my aged uncle Arly, sitting on a
heap of barley". It would be wonderful to read the whole poem
again.'*

GOING ON AN ERRAND
Anonymous

A pound of tea at one and three
And a pot of raspberry jam
Two new laid eggs, a dozen pegs
And a pound of rashers of ham.

I'll say it over all the way
And then I'm sure not to forget
For if I chance to bring things wrong
My Mother gets in such a sweat.

A pound of tea at one and three
And a pot of raspberry jam
Two new laid eggs, a dozen pegs
And a pound of rashers of ham.

There in the hay the children play
They're having such fine fun
I'll go there too that's what I'll do
As soon as my errands are done.

A pound of tea at one and three
A pot of ... er ... new laid jam
Two raspberry eggs with a dozen pegs
And a pound of rashers of ham.

There's Teddy White flying his kite
He thinks himself grand I declare
I'd like to make it fly up sky high
Ever so much higher than the old church spire

And then – but there

A pound of three at one and tea
A pot of new laid jam
Two dozen eggs, some raspberry pegs
And a pound of rashers of ham.

Now here's the shop outside I'll stop
And run my orders through again
I haven't forgot – it's better not
It shows I'm pretty quick that's plain.

A pound of tea at one and three
A dozen of raspberry ham
A pot of eggs with a dozen pegs
And a rasher of new laid jam.

*A splendid piece of nonsense, very suitable for Forgotten Verse.
To judge from the price of tea, one would estimate that it was
written around 1900.*

THE MAD GARDENER'S SONG
by Lewis Carroll

He thought he saw an Elephant,
That practised on a fife:
He looked again, and found it was
A letter from his wife.
'At length I realise,' he said,
'The bitterness of Life!'

He thought he saw a Bufffalo
Upon the chimney-piece:
He looked again, and found it was
His Sister's Husband's Niece.
'Unless you leave this house,' he said,
'I'll send for the Police!'

He thought he saw a Rattlesnake
That questioned him in Greek:
He looked again, and found it was
The Middle of Next Week.
'The one thing I regret,' he said,
'Is that it cannot speak!'

He thought he saw a Banker's Clerk
Descending from the bus:
He looked again, and found it was
A Hippopotamus.
'If this should stay to dine,' he said,
'There won't be much for us!'

He thought he saw a Kangaroo
That worked a coffee-mill:
He looked again, and found it was
A Vegetable-Pill.
'Were I to swallow this,' he said,
'I should be very ill!'

He thought he saw a Coach-and-Four
That stood beside his bed:
He looked again, and found it was
A Bear without a Head.
'Poor thing,' he said, 'poor silly thing!
It's waiting to be fed!'

He thought he saw an Albatross
That fluttered round the lamp:
He looked again, and found it was
A Penny-Postage Stamp.
'You'd best be getting home,' he said:
'The nights are very damp!'

He thought he saw a Garden-Door
That opened with a key:
He looked again, and found it was
A Double Rule of Three:
'And all its mystery,' he said,
'Is clear as day to me!'

He thought he saw a Argument
That proved he was the Pope:
He looked again, and found it was
A Bar of Mottled Soap.
'A fact so dread,' he faintly said,
'Extinguishes all hope!'

This comes from Sylvie And Bruno, *one of Lewis Carroll's lesser-known works, and occurs a verse at a time at various points in the story.*

ABDUL ABULBUL AMIR
by William Percy French

The sons of the Prophet are brave men and bold
And quite unaccustomed to fear,
But the bravest by far in the ranks of the Shah,
Was Abdul Abulbul Amir.

If you wanted a man to encourage the van,
Or harass the foe from the rear,
Storm fort or redoubt, you had only to shout
For Abdul Abulbul Amir.

Now the heroes were plenty and well known to fame
In the troops that were led by the Czar,
And the bravest of these was a man by the name
Of Ivan Skavinsky Skavar.

One day this bold Russian, he shouldered his gun
And donned his most truculent sneer,
Downtown he did go where he trod on the toe
Of Abdul Abulbul Amir.

'Young man,' quoth Abdul, 'has life grown so dull
That you wish to end your career?
Vile infidel, know, you have trod on the toe
Of Abdul Abulbul Amir.

'So take your last look at the sunshine and brook
And send your regrets to the Czar
For by this I imply, you are going to die,
Count Ivan Skavinsky Skavar.'

Then this bold Mameluke drew his trusty skibouk,
Singing, 'Allah! Il Allah! Al-lah!'
And with murderous intent he ferociously went
For Ivan Skavinsky Skavar.

They parried and thrust, they side-stepped and cussed,
Of blood they spilled a great part;
The philologist blokes, who seldom crack jokes,
Say that hash was first made on the spot.

They fought all that night neath the pale yellow moon;
The din, it was heard from afar,
And huge multitudes came, so great was the fame,
Of Abdul and Ivan Skavar.

As Abdul's long knife was extracting the life,
In fact he was shouting, 'Huzzah!'
He felt himself struck by that wily Calmuck,
Count Ivan Skavinsky Skavar.

The Sultan drove by in his red-breasted fly,
Expecting the victor to cheer,
But he only drew nigh to hear the last sigh,
Of Abdul Abulbul Amir.

There's a tomb rises up where the Blue Danube rolls,
And graved there in characters clear,
Is, 'Stranger, when passing, oh pray for the soul
Of Abdul Abulbul Amir.'

A splash in the Black Sea one dark moonless night
Caused ripples to spread wide and far,
It was made by a sack fitting close to the back,
Of Ivan Skavinsky Skavar.

A Muscovite maiden her lone vigil keeps,
'Neath the light of the cold northern star,
And the name that she murmurs in vain as she weeps,
Is Ivan Skavinsky Skavar.

William Percy French (1854–1920)
One of Ireland's foremost songwriters and entertainers, as well as being a watercolour painter, French was less successful at business: he sold Abdul Abulbul Amir for only £5 to a shrewd publisher, and it later became hugely famous. You can see a statue of William Percy French on a park bench in the town of Ballyjamesduff in Ireland, in honour of his famous song, 'Come Back Paddy Reilly To Ballyjamesduff'.

10.

Inspirational Verse

GREAT, WIDE, BEAUTIFUL, WONDERFUL WORLD
by William Brighty Rands

Great, wide, beautiful, wonderful World,
With the wonderful water round you curled,
And the wonderful grass upon your breast –
World, you are beautifully drest.

The wonderful air is over me,
And the wonderful wind is shaking the tree,
It walks on the water, and whirls the mills,
And talks to itself on the tops of the hills.

You friendly Earth! how far do you go,
With the wheat-fields that nod and the rivers that flow,
With cities and gardens, and cliffs, and isles,
And people upon you for thousands of miles?

Ah, you are so great, and I am so small,
I tremble to think of you, World, at all;
And yet, when I said my prayers to-day,
A whisper inside me seemed to say,
'You are more than the Earth, though you are such a dot:
You can love and think, and the Earth cannot!'

---

*Rands' religious beliefs and love of nature come through strongly
in this, one of his best-loved verses. He was an eccentric
character, the poorly educated son of a candle maker who picked
up most of his knowledge by browsing second-hand bookstalls.
His kind nature came through in his first job in a solicitor's
office, when he resigned because he found it too upsetting
serving writs on poor tradesmen*

A MAN OF WORDS AND NOT OF DEEDS
Anonymous

A man of words and not of deeds
Is like a garden full of weeds
And when the weeds begin to grow
It's like a garden full of snow
And when the snow begins to fall
It's like a bird upon the wall
And when the bird away does fly
It's like an eagle in the sky
And when the sky begins to roar
It's like a lion at the door
And when the door begins to crack
It's like a stick across your back
And when your back begins to smart
It's like a penknife in your heart
And when your heart begins to bleed
You're dead, and dead, and dead indeed.

This poem allegedly was inspired by a work by Elizabethan writer John Fletcher. The phrase 'deeds, not words' appears in Act III of his Lover's Progress.

SOMEBODY'S MOTHER
by Mary Dow Brine

The woman was old and ragged and grey
And bent with the chill of the Winter's day.
The street was wet with a recent snow
And the woman's feet were aged and slow.
She stood at the crossing and waited long,
Alone, uncared for, amid the throng
Of human beings who passed her by
Nor heeded the glance of her anxious eyes.
Down the street, with laughter and shout,
Glad in the freedom of 'school let out,'
Came the boys like a flock of sheep,
Hailing the snow piled white and deep.
Past the woman so old and grey
Hastened the children on their way.
Nor offered a helping hand to her –
So meek, so timid, afraid to stir
Lest the carriage wheels or the horses' feet
Should crowd her down in the slippery street.
At last came one of the merry troop,
The gayest lad of all the group;
He paused beside her and whispered low,
'I'll help you cross, if you wish to go.'
Her aged hand on his strong young arm
She placed, and so, without hurt or harm,
He guided the trembling feet along,
Proud that his own were firm and strong.

Then back again to his friends he went,
His young heart happy and well content.
'She's somebody's mother, boys, you know,
For all she's aged and poor and slow,
And I hope some fellow will lend a hand
To help my mother, you understand,
If ever she's poor and old and grey,
And her own dear boy is far away.'
'Somebody's mother' bowed low her head
In her home that night, and the prayer she said
Was 'God be kind to the noble boy,
Who is somebody's son, and pride and joy!'

Mary Dow Brine (1816–1913)
*Mary Dow Brine was a native of New York, and is most famous
for this poem – though she also wrote lullabies.*

*We constantly receive requests for this verse, which is a
wonderful evocation of traditional values and respect for the
elderly, with a touching and unexpected meeting across the
generations.*

THE FIFTIETH BIRTHDAY OF AGASSIZ
by Henry Wadsworth Longfellow

It was fifty years ago
In the pleasant month of May,
In the beautiful Pays de Vaud,
A child in its cradle lay.

And Nature, the old nurse, took
The child upon her knee,
Saying: 'Here is a story-book
Thy Father has written for thee.'

'Come, wander with me,' she said,
'Into regions yet untrod;
And read what is still unread
In the manuscripts of God.'

And he wandered away and away
With Nature, the dear old nurse,
Who sang to him night and day
The rhymes of the universe.

And whenever the way seemed long,
Or his heart began to fail,
She would sing a more wonderful song,
Or tell a more marvellous tale.

So she keeps him still a child,
And will not let him go,
Though at times his heart beats wild
For the beautiful Pays de Vaud;

Though at times he hears in his dreams
The Ranz des Vaches of old,
And the rush of mountain streams
From glaciers clear and cold;

And the mother at home says, 'Hark!
For his voice I listen and yearn;
It is growing late and dark,
And my boy does not return!'

This poem was written in 1857 by Longfellow to celebrate the fiftieth birthday of the zoologist Louis Agassiz. It is a wonderful evocation of a scientist's lifelong rapture with the workings of Nature, as appropriate to read to a child as to a fifty-year-old looking back on his scientific life.

LANDING OF THE PILGRIM FATHERS
by Felicia Dorothea Hemans

The breaking waves dashed high
On a stern and rock-bound coast,
And the woods, against a stormy sky,
Their giant branches tos't;

And the heavy night hung dark
The hills and water o'er,
When a band of exiles moored their bark
On the wild New England shore.

Not as the conqueror comes,
They, the true-hearted, came;
Not with the roll of the stirring drums,
And the trumpet that sings of fame;

Not as the flying come,
In silence and in fear, –
They shook the depths of the desert's gloom
With their hymns of lofty cheer.

Amidst the storm they sang,
And the stars heard and the sea;
And the sounding aisles of the dim woods rang
To the anthem of the free.

The ocean-eagle soared
From his nest by the white wave's foam,
And the rocking pines of the forest roared –
This was their welcome home!

There were men with hoary hair
Amidst that pilgrim band:
Why had they come to wither there,
Away from their childhood's land?

There was woman's fearless eye,
Lit by her deep love's truth;
There was manhood's brow serenely high,
And the fiery heart of youth.

What sought they thus afar?
Bright jewels of the mine?
The wealth of the seas? the spoils of war? –
They sought a faith's pure shrine!

Ay, call it holy ground,
The soil where first they trod!
They have left unstained what there they found –
Freedom to worship God!

An account of the voyage of the Mayflower in 1620, when the pilgrims brought their ship into what came to be known as Cape Cod harbour and a band of sixteen men, led by Captain Miles Standish, landed to explore the shore. This desire for freedom to worship God as they pleased was the reason for the founding of the first colony.

THE SLAVE'S DREAM
by Henry Wadsworth Longfellow

Beside the ungathered rice he lay,
His sickle in his hand;
His breast was bare, his matted hair
Was buried in the sand.
Again, in the mist and shadow of sleep,
He saw his Native Land.

Wide through the landscape of his dreams
The lordly Niger flowed;
Beneath the palm-trees on the plain
Once more a king he strode;
And heard the tinkling caravans
Descending the mountain road.

He saw once more his dark-eyed queen
Among her children stand;
They clasped his neck, they kissed his cheeks,
They held him by the hand! –
A tear burst from the sleeper's lids
And fell into the sand.

And then at furious speed he rode
Along the Niger's bank;
His bridle-reins were golden chains,
And with a martial clank,
At each leap he could feel his scabbard of steel
Smiting his stallion's flank.

Before him, like a blood-red flag,
The bright flamingoes flew;
From morn till night he followed their flight,
O'er plains where the tamarind grew,
Till he saw the roofs of Caffre huts,
And the ocean rose to view.

At night he heard the lion roar,
And the hyena scream,
And the river-horse, as he crushed the reeds
Beside some hidden stream;
And it passed, like a glorious roll of drums,
Through the triumph of his dream.

The forest, with their myriad tongues,
Shouted of liberty,
And the Blast of the Desert cried aloud,
With a voice so wild and free,
That he started in his sleep and smiled
At their tempestuous glee.

He did not feel the driver's whip,
Nor the burning heat of day;
For Death had illumined the Land of Sleep,
And his lifeless body lay
A worn-out fetter, that the soul
Had broken and thrown away!

This was one of a group entitled Poems on Slavery written by Longfellow in 1842. It is one of the most frequently requested of all our Forgotten Verses, studied long ago at school and now forgotten apart from a few lines.

IF
by Rudyard Kipling

If you can keep your head when all about you
Are losing theirs and blaming it on you,
If you can trust yourself when all men doubt you,
But make allowance for their doubting too;

If you can wait and not be tired by waiting,
Or being lied about, don't deal in lies,
Or being hated, don't give way to hating,
And yet don't look too good, nor talk too wise:

If you can dream – and not make dreams your master;
If you can think – and not make thoughts your aim;
If you can meet with Triumph and Disaster
And treat those two impostors just the same;

If you can bear to hear the truth you've spoken
Twisted by knaves to make a trap for fools,
Or watch the things you gave your life to broken,
And stoop and build 'em up with wornout tools:

If you can make one heap of all your winnings
And risk it on one turn of pitch-and-toss,
And lose, and start again at your beginnings
And never breathe a word about your loss;

If you can force your heart and nerve and sinew
To serve your turn long after they are gone,
And so hold on when there is nothing in you
Except the Will which says to them: 'Hold on!'

If you can talk with crowds and keep your virtue,
Or walk with kings – nor lose the common touch,
If neither foes nor loving friends can hurt you,
If all men count with you, but none too much;

If you can fill the unforgiving minute
With sixty seconds' worth of distance run –
Yours is the Earth and everything that's in it,
And – which is more – you'll be a Man my son!

This was voted the nation's favourite poem in a BBC poll in 1995.

UPHILL
by Christina Georgina Rossetti

Does the road wind uphill all the way?
Yes, to the very end.
Will the day's journey take the whole long day?
From morn to night, my friend.

But is there for the night a resting-place?
A roof for when the slow, dark hours begin.
May not the darkness hide it from my face?
You cannot miss that inn.

Shall I meet other wayfarers at night?
Those who have gone before.
Then must I knock, or call when just in sight?
They will not keep you waiting at that door.

Shall I find comfort, travel-sore and weak?
Of labour you shall find the sum.
Will there be beds for me and all who seek?
Yea, beds for all who come.

Christina Georgina Rossetti (1830–94)
Sister of the well-known artist Dante Gabriel Rossetti, Christina
began writing at an early age but was not published until she
was thirty-one. Her first book was Goblin Market And Other
Verses *which was so well received that she was soon described*
as the 'female laureate'.

11.

Animals

THE ROOKS
by Jane Euphemia Browne

The rooks are building on the trees;
   They build there every spring:
     'Caw, caw,' is all they say,
    For none of them can sing.

They're up before the break of day,
    And up till late at night;
   For they must labour busily
     As long as it is light.

And many a crooked stick they bring,
    And many a slender twig,
And many a tuft of moss, until
    Their nests are round and big.

    'Caw, caw!' Oh, what a noise
    They make in rainy weather!
Good children always speak by turns,
    But rooks all talk together.

Jane Euphemia Browne (1811–98)
Specialising in children's verse about nature, Jane Euphemia
Browne published many of her works under the pseudonym 'Aunt
Effie'.

DUCK'S DITTY
by Kenneth Grahame

All along the backwater,
Through the rushes tall,
Ducks are a-dabbling,
Up tails all!

Ducks' tails, drakes' tails,
Yellow feet a-quiver,
Yellow bills all out of sight
Busy in the river!

Slushy green undergrowth
Where the roach swim –
Here we keep our larder,
Cool and full and dim.

Everyone for what he likes!
We like to be
Heads down, tails up,
Dabbling free!

High in the blue above
Swifts whirl and call—
We are down a-dabbling
Up tails all!

Kenneth Grahame (1859–1932)
Grahame was born in Edinburgh and worked at the Bank of
England until his retirement in 1907. In his spare time, he wrote
the children's classic The Wind In The Willows, *from which this*
poem is taken, and many short stories, including 'The Reluctant
Dragon', which was later made into a Disney film.

THE AGE OF A HORSE
Anonymous

To tell the age of any horse
Inspect the lower jaw, of course.
The six front teeth the tale will tell,
And every doubt and fear dispel.

Two middle nippers you behold
Before the colt is two weeks old.
Before eight weeks two more will come;
Eight months the corners cut the gum.

The outside grooves will disappear
From middle two in just one year;
In two years from the second pair;
In three years 'corners', too, are bare.

At two the middle 'nippers' drop.
At three the second pair can't stop.
When four years old the third pair goes.
At five a full new set he shows.

The deep black spots will pass from view
At six years from the middle two;
The second pair at seven years;
At eight the spot each corner clears.

From middle 'nippers' upper jaw
At nine the black spots will withdraw.
The second pair at ten are bright;
Eleven finds the corners light.

As time goes on, the horsemen know,
The oval teeth three-sided grow.
The old horse has more 'whoa' than 'get'
We keep him only for a pet.

*An anonymous oddity, requested by Josephine Underwood of
Kendal. 'This was told to me by my granddad more than fifty
years ago, but I have lost the opening verses. The poem told how
you can tell the age of a horse by its teeth, which my granddad,
being a blacksmith, probably found very useful.'*

THE LITTLE DOG'S DAY
by Rupert Brooke

All in the town were still asleep,
When the sun came up with a shout and a leap.
In the lonely streets unseen by man,
A little dog danced. And the day began.

All his life he'd been good, as far as he could,
And the poor little beast had done all that he should.
But this morning he swore, by Odin and Thor
And the Canine Valhalla he'd stand it no more!

So his prayer he got granted to do just what he wanted,
Prevented by none, for the space of one day.
'Jam incipiebo, sedere facebo,'
In dog-Latin he quoth, 'Euge! sophos! hurray!'

He fought with the he-dogs, and winked at the she-dogs,
A thing that had never been heard of before.
'For the stigma of gluttony, I care not a button!' he
Cried, and ate all he could swallow and more.

He took sinewy lumps from the shins of old frumps,
And mangled the errand-boys when he could get 'em.
He shammed furious rabies, and bit all the babies,
And followed the cats up the trees, and then ate 'em!'

They thought 'twas the devil was holding a revel,
And sent for the parson to drive him away;
For the town never knew such a hullabaloo
As that little dog raised till the end of that day.

When the blood-red sun had gone burning down,
And the lights were lit in the little town,
Outside, in the gloom of the twilight grey,
The little dog died when he'd had his day.

'I have been trying to track down a poem for years now. I think it was called "The little dog's day". We had to learn it at school but the only verse I remember ends, "A little dog danced and the day began". I think it has a sad ending but it would be marvellous if you could find it for me.' (Patricia Palmer, Cornwall)

SONG – THE OWL
by Alfred, Lord Tennyson

When cats run home and light is come,
And dew is cold upon the ground,
And the far-off stream is dumb,
And the whirring sail goes round,
And the whirring sail goes round;
Alone and warming his five wits,
The white owl in the belfry sits.

When merry milkmaids click the latch,
And rarely smells the new-mown hay,
And the cock hath sung beneath the thatch
Twice or thrice his roundelay,
Twice or thrice his roundelay;
Alone and warming his five wits,
The white owl in the belfry sits.

SECOND SONG TO THE SAME

Thy tuwhits are lull'd I wot,
Thy tuwhoos of yesternight,
Which upon the dark afloat,
So took echo with delight,
So took echo with delight,
That her voice untuneful grown,
Wears all day a fainter tone.

I would mock thy chaunt anew;
But I cannot mimick it;
Not a whit of thy tuwhoo,
Thee to woo to thy tuwhit,
Thee to woo to thy tuwhit,
With a lengthen'd loud halloo,
Tuwhoo, tuwhit, tuwhit, tuwhoo-o-o.

This was requested by Sheila Terry, whose sole memory was of the lines 'When merry milkmaids click the latch, and rarely smells the new mown hay.'

THE CAMEL'S HUMP
by Rudyard Kipling

The Camel's hump is an ugly lump
Which well you may see at the Zoo;
But uglier yet is the hump we get
From having too little to do.

Kiddies and grown-ups too-oo-oo,
If we haven't enough to do-oo-oo,
We get the hump –
Cameelious hump –
The hump that is black and blue!

We climb out of bed with a frouzly head
And a snarly-yarly voice.
We shiver and scowl and we grunt and we growl
At our bath and our boots and our toys;

And there ought to be a corner for me
(And I know there is one for you)
When we get the hump –
Cameelious hump –
The hump that is black and blue!

The cure for this ill is not to sit still,
Or frowst with a book by the fire;
But to take a large hoe and a shovel also,
And dig till you gently perspire;

And then you will find that the sun and the wind,
And the Djinn of the Garden too,
Have lifted the hump –
The horrible hump –
The hump that is black and blue!

I get it as well as you-oo-oo –
If I haven't enough to do-oo-oo –
We all get hump –
Cameelious hump –
Kiddies and grown-ups too!

This verse appears at the end of Kipling's story, 'How The Camel Got Its Hump', in his Just So Stories. *It has been requested by numerous* Daily Express *readers.*

FIDELITY
by William Wordsworth

A barking sound the Shepherd hears,
A cry as of a dog or fox;
He halts – and searches with his eyes
Among the scattered rocks:
And now at distance can discern
A stirring in a brake of fern;
And instantly a dog is seen,
Glancing through that covert green.

The Dog is not of mountain breed;
Its motions, too, are wild and shy;
With something, as the Shepherd thinks,
Unusual in its cry:
Nor is there any one in sight
All round, in hollow or on height;
Nor shout, nor whistle strikes his ear;
What is the creature doing here?

It was a cove, a huge recess,
That keeps, till June, December's snow;
A lofty precipice in front,
A silent tarn below!
Far in the bosom of Helvellyn,
Remote from public road or dwelling,
Pathway, or cultivated land;
From trace of human foot or hand.

There sometimes doth a leaping fish
Send through the tarn a lonely cheer;
The crags repeat the raven's croak,
In symphony austere;
Thither the rainbow comes – the cloud –
And mists that spread the flying shroud;
And sunbeams; and the sounding blast,
That, if it could, would hurry past;
But that enormous barrier holds it fast.

Not free from boding thoughts, a while
The Shepherd stood; then makes his way
O'er rocks and stones, following the Dog
As quickly as he may;
Nor far had gone before he found
A human skeleton on the ground;
The appalled Discoverer with a sigh
Looks round, to learn the history.

From those abrupt and perilous rocks
The Man had fallen, that place of fear!
At length upon the Shepherd's mind
It breaks, and all is clear:
He instantly recalled the name,
And who he was, and whence he came;
Remembered, too, the very day
On which the Traveller passed this way.

But hear a wonder, for whose sake
This lamentable tale I tell!
A lasting monument of words
This wonder merits well.
The Dog, which still was hovering nigh,
Repeating the same timid cry,
This Dog, had been through three months' space
A dweller in that savage place.

Yes, proof was plain that, since the day
When this ill-fated Traveller died,
The Dog had watched about the spot,
Or by his master's side:
How nourished here through such long time
He knows, who gave that love sublime;
And gave that strength of feeling, great
Above all human estimate!

The poem was inspired by an incident in the 1820s, when a climber called Charles Gough fell while climbing Helvellyn Mountain and his terrier kept watch over his body for three months. The event was also commemorated in a painting by Landseer and another poem by Sir Walter Scott.

THE REVERIE OF POOR SUSAN
by William Wordsworth

At the corner of Wood Street, when daylight appears,
Hangs a Thrush that sings loud, it has sung for three years:
Poor Susan has passed by the spot, and has heard
In the silence of morning the song of the Bird.

'Tis a note of enchantment; what ails her? She sees
A mountain ascending, a vision of trees;
Bright volumes of vapour through Lothbury glide,
And a river flows on through the vale of Cheapside.

Green pastures she views in the midst of the dale,
Down which she so often has tripped with her pail;
And a single small cottage, a nest like a dove's,
The one only dwelling on earth that she loves.

She looks, and her heart is in heaven: but they fade,
The mist and the river, the hill and the shade:
The stream will not flow, and the hill will not rise,
And the colours have all passed away from her eyes!

This was requested by Louise Jefferson from London, who asked to be reminded of 'a poem I heard in school, some fifty years ago'.

THE OWL CRITIC
by James T Fields

'Who stuffed that white owl?' No one spoke in the shop:
The barber was busy, and he couldn't stop;
The customers, waiting their turns, were all reading
The 'Daily,' the 'Herald,' the 'Post,' little heeding
The young man who blurted out such a blunt question;
Not one raised a head or even made a suggestion;
And the barber kept on shaving.

'Don't you see, Mr. Brown,'
Cried the youth, with a frown,
'How wrong the whole thing is,
How preposterous each wing is,
How flattened the head is, how jammed down the neck is –
In short, the whole owl, what an ignorant wreck 'tis!
I make no apology;
I've learned owl-eology.
I've passed days and nights in a hundred collections,
And cannot be blinded to any deflections
Arising from unskillful fingers that fail
To stuff a bird right, from his beak to his tail.
Mister Brown! Mister Brown!
Do take that bird down,
Or you'll soon be the laughing-stock all over town!'
And the barber kept on shaving.

'I've studied owls,
And other night fowls,
And I tell you
What I know to be true:
An owl cannot roost
With his limbs so unloosed;

No owl in this world
Ever had his claws curled,
Ever had his legs slanted,
Ever had his bill canted,
Ever had his neck screwed
Into that attitude.
He can't do it, because
'Tis against all bird laws.
Anatomy teaches,
Ornithology preaches
An owl has a toe
That can't turn out so!
I've made the white owl my study for years,
And to see such a job almost moves me to tears!
Mister Brown, I'm amazed
You should be so gone crazed
As to put up a bird
In that posture absurd!
To look at that owl really brings on a dizziness;
The man who stuffed him don't know half his business!'
And the barber kept on shaving.

'Examine those eyes.
I'm filled with surpprise
Taxidermists should pass
Off on you such poor glass;
So unnatural they seem
They'd make Audubon scream,
And John Burroughs laugh
To encounter such chaff.
Do take that bird down;
Have him stuffed again, Brown!'
And the barber kept on shaving.

'With some sawdust and bark
I could stuff in the dark
An owl better than that.
I could make an old hat
Look more like an owl
Than that horrid fowl,
Stuck up there so stiff like a side of coarse leather.
In fact, about him there's not one natural feather.'

Just then, with a wink and a sly normal lurch,
The owl, very gravely, got down from his perch,
Walked around and regarded his fault-finding critic
(Who thought he was stuffed) with a glance analytic,
And then fairly hooted, as if he should say:
'Your learning's at fault this time, anyway;
Don't waste it again on a live bird, I pray.
I'm an owl; you're another. Sir Critic, good-day!'
And the barber kept on shaving.

James Thomas Fields (1817–81)
Publisher. essayist and author, Fields worked in Boston,
Massachusetts, and was a leading figure in the American literary
world. Among his poetry, his best-known work is 'The Owl
Critic', a satire on the vanity of critics.

Indexes

INDEX OF FIRST LINES

INDEX OF POETS

William Hartston has been writing for the *Daily Express* since 1998, contributing the daily Beachcomber column, as well as a variety of columns on useless information (including the daily Ten Things You Didn't Know About...), the Saturday Briefing page, and, of course, Forgotten Verse. He also contributes a number of the paper's puzzles, an expertise he attributes to a wasted youth. He has written extensively on the game of chess, and was British Chess Champion in 1973 and 1975.

THE TOP TEN

When Forgotten Verse began in the *Daily Express*, we expected requests to concentrate on the poems that we all learnt at school, yet the diversity of poems asked for has been astonishing. Each post brings many more requests for previously unmentioned items, though a few titles and lines crop up again and again. Here are the ten most requested poems of all, each asked for dozens of times. You might call them the Ten Most Forgotten Poems in the English language.

1. *Meg Merrilies* by John Keats

2. *Abou Ben Adhem* by James Henry Leigh Hunt

3. *The Slave's Dream* by Henry Wadsworth Longfellow

4. *The Pedlar's Caravan* by William Brighty Rands

5. *The Months* by Sara Coleridge

6. *Big Steamers* by Rudyard Kipling

7. *From A Railway Carriage* by Robert Louis Stevenson

8. *Somebody's Mother* by Mary Dow Brine

9. *The Soldier* by Rupert Brooke

10. *Innominatus* by Sir Walter Scott